POEMS AND SKETCHES OF E. B. WHITE

POEMS AND

SKETCHES OF

E. B. White

1817

HARPER & ROW, PUBLISHERS, New York
Cambridge, Philadelphia, San Francisco, London,
Mexico City, São Paulo, Sydney

POEMS AND SKETCHES OF E. B. WHITE. Copyright 1925, 1926, 1928, 1929, 1930, 1931, 1932, 1933, 1934, 1935, 1936, 1937, 1938, 1939, 1940, 1941, 1942, 1943, 1944, 1945, 1946, 1947, 1948, 1949, 1950, 1951, 1952, 1954, © 1955, 1956, 1957, 1958, 1959, 1967, 1969, 1970, 1976, 1981 by E. B. White. All rights reserved. Printed in the United States of America. No part of this book may be used or reproduced in any manner whatsoever without written permission except in the case of brief quotations embodied in critical articles and reviews. For information address Harper & Row, Publishers, Inc., 10 East 53rd Street, New York, N.Y. 10022. Published simultaneously in Canada by Fitzhenry & Whiteside Limited, Toronto.

FIRST EDITION

Designer: Sidney Feinberg

Library of Congress Cataloging in Publication Data
White, E. B. (Elwyn Brooks), 1899–
  Poems and sketches of E.B. White.
  I. Title.
PS3545.H5187A6 1981   811'.52   81-47240
ISBN 0-06-014900-0
                                                              AACR2

81 82 83 84 85 10 9 8 7 6 5 4 3 2 1

For Corona

Contents

Preface

This is a fraudulent book. Here I am presented as a poet, when it is common knowledge that I have never received my accreditation papers admitting me to the ranks of American poets. Having lived happily all my life as a non-poet who occasionally breaks into song, I have no wish at this late hour to change either my status or my habits even if I were capable of doing so, and I clearly am not. The life of a non-poet is an agreeable one: he feels no obligation to mingle with other writers of verse to exchange sensitivities, no compulsion to visit the "Y" to read from his own works, no need to travel the wine-and-cheese circuit, where the word "poet" carries the aroma of magic and ladies creep up from behind carrying ballpoint pens and sprigs of asphodel.

At an early age, it would appear, I fell into questionable habits: I liked to rhyme one word with another, liked to fashion lines that bore some relation to other lines in the same stanza, liked to proceed in a strict, or almost strict, metrical manner. This sort of thing is rare nowadays. The poet of today is neither a lyricist nor a cutup, he is a serious artist bent on expressing an emotional thought in a straightforward, if sometimes uninteresting, way.

Not long ago, I happened to come across an explanation of another weakness of mine as a poet. This was a passage from a speech given at New York University by Louise Bogan some years before her death. She said, "Openness and sincerity will protect the poet from . . . small emotions with which poetry should not, and cannot, deal." Well, there you have it. When I was young, I thought of myself as open and sincere, but I'm quite sure I never tried to gauge in advance the size of an emotion to discover whether it was deserving of my time and attention. From the evidence in this book it is clear that if an emotion hit me, however tiny the little fellow was, I leapt into action without sizing the situation up—without cooling myself off to wait for a bigger fish. This can be damaging, if a poet is headed for greatness.

Perhaps it all comes down to my having been born into the wrong century. My instincts, I suspect, are those of the jongleur, the troubadour, the minstrel, the minnesinger—those busy entertainers and news commentators of the Middle Ages. I think I would have felt at home among such fellows; in early times I might have made out all right. A medieval household wasn't complete without its poet-in-residence, and in some cases the poet was paid lavishly. I would have liked that. Minstrels were frowned on by the Church in England, but were made welcome in homes and taverns where people were starved for television. The minstrel carried the news, and I would have liked that. (Several of the poems in this book, I notice, carry the news.) The minstrel's songs were often ribald and indecent, and I would have enjoyed that. Among the minnesingers —the German lyric poets of the twelfth and thirteenth centuries—love songs were the commonest expression, the homage paid by a knight to his mistress. The poems were usually sung in open court, and a minnesinger might have his private harper. Wouldn't I have loved *that!* But a man can't pick his century: he must operate in whatever time slot he gets dropped into by his unthinking mother.

Despite all attempts to pin him down, the poet is still as mysterious as he is prevalent. Surely one out of every three persons is a poet—either secretly or openly. There is no problem here, because poets (unlike novelists and playwrights) can be self-proclaimed. I read recently of a woman who traveled to a distant town with her Muse and set up shop in a friendly restaurant. She simply put a large sign saying POET in the front window, and the place soon filled up with customers ready and eager to see a poet in the flesh and hear her recite. Back in the New Deal days, when someone told Robert Frost that there were six hundred poets working for the W.P.A., he snapped, "There haven't been six hundred poets in human history." But Frost was whistling in the dark—he was defending his territorial rights in a jungle world. You can bet, knowing Frost, that he was also privately listing himself among the ones that had made the grade.

To me, poetry is what is memorable, and a poet is a fellow or girl who lets drop a line that gets remembered in the morning. Poetry turns up in unexpected places, in unguarded moments. I have yet to encounter the line (from a song in *Oklahoma!*) "All the sounds of the earth are like music" without being brought to the edge of tears. Yet when I encounter another familiar simile by another Broadway songwriter, "A pretty girl is like a melody," I am entertained but not moved. The whole business is, and will continue to be, mysterious, and I should never have brought it up.

As for the sketches in this book: "Sketch" is a word that covers a lot of ground. Webster defines it as "a brief, light, or informal short story, essay, or other literary composition." I have used the word as a handy umbrella over everything in this collection that is not a poem.

Many of these poems and sketches were written a long time ago—so long ago, in fact, that they will come as a surprise (I hope an agreeable surprise) to a new generation of readers who didn't have the good sense to be alive when I was hard at work. A number of them are from early collections that are no longer in print. Several have never been between covers, a few have never been published. Some of the sketches started life as editorials in *The New Yorker*; for this book I have dropped the editorial "we" and substituted the more forthright "I." "Memoirs of a Master" appeared in *The New Yorker* but not over my name—I used a pseudonym. The poem called "Reading Room," which was inspired by hours spent in the New York Public Library, where I often went not to read but to write, traveled many miles in search of a publisher—I sent it to everybody I could think of, but it always came back. On rereading it, I couldn't find anything much wrong with it, so I closed my eyes and dropped it into the enormous pile of raw material from which a selection would be made, to see what would happen. I still feel a sentimental attachment to the Library, still have a sense of indebtedness.

I suspect that informality is a key to this collection. Putting it together—a selection from hundreds of pieces, old and recent—was comparable to choosing seven children from a class of fifty to take part in a school play. Faced with this touchy task, my editor at Harper & Row and I began with a bold move: we left town. We fetched up, heavily laden, two thousand miles away, under a Royal Poinciana tree whose seed pods were a dirty brown and about the size of a policeman's billy. Our workroom in this exotic setting boasted a large, round table, and on this we dumped my incredible accumulation of poems and sketches in all stages of disrepair—as formidable and disorderly a pile as I have ever seen. Mornings, we met at the round table and started pitching things into one of the three boxes labelled YES, NO, and MAYBE, which I had deployed on the floor within chucking distance, as you would place a hat into which to toss playing cards.

The first thing that became apparent was that the NO box was filling up with astonishing rapidity—manuscripts and clip sheets sailed through the air and with one or two exceptions landed in NO. The exceptions went into MAYBE. I sneaked a look into the YES box after an hour or two: it was empty.

There was a lumpy couch in the room, and I went over and lay down, staring at the ceiling and wondering where it was all going to end. I think I was almost asleep when the stillness was broken by a sudden peal of laughter—the first explicit sound of the day. I sat up in time to see something flutter into the YES box, and I felt that I had snatched the brass ring on the merry-go-round.

For a while, while the book was being assembled, I debated with myself whether to bring up the awkward matter of my poetical stature. Finally I decided to make a clean breast of it. I told my editor that I had never been accredited.

"I can fix that," she replied. "Instead of having a poetry section and a prose section, we will scatter the poems around in the text, intermingling them with the other stuff. We'll conceal the poems in the underbrush."

I fell in with this slick scheme right away. And that's how the book got put together—an amusing exercise in intermingling. I don't suppose it will work, but it's one more queer book in a long succession, and I have had a very nice time along the way.

—E.B.W.

I

INSCRUTABLE

AND

LOVELY TOWN

THE HOTEL
OF THE TOTAL STRANGER

With the train having arrived and the blurred terminal having been safely passed through and the porter ahead with the bags and then the bags first into the cab and the question "Where to?" obediently and correctly answered, Mr. Volente settled back into the leather seat with one foot on his luggage and his head now resting back and his gaze fixed upward through the open skylight, the buildings crouching over him and sweeping by. There is no earliness, said Mr. Volente without saying anything, quite like the earliness of a city morning in the great heat of summer, the audible heat, the visible heat, odorous and vaporous and terrible and seductive. He could still feel against his toe the quick nudge of the metal plate at the top of the escalator, hitting his toe at the end of the ascent as though it (the stationary element) were actually the moving element, as though the terminal had slipped itself under his foot, he being rigid, still, quiescent, the terminal being fluent, restless, and suddenly buoyant and he suddenly floor-borne.

The Hotel of the Total Stranger, he had said to the driver, Max Weinraub, and the door had closed and the hand of Weinraub had, reaching back, lowered the flag on the meter and the yellow flight had begun toward the known destination, the predictable hotel room (although it might be almost any number, still always the same room—it might be 302, or it might be 907 on the ninth floor, or it might be Number 1411 which would be a hard number to remember and he would be always asking for the wrong key perhaps), but it would be the familiar room just the same with the, Mr. Volente was sure, same things in it, no matter what number. It would have first the airless abandoned feeling and then the windows flung up by the boy dropping the bags and instantly the infiltration of the noise and the heat and the life and the pigeon on the sill straightening its feathers. The walls would be apple green, the paneling (apple green) decorative on the wall being formed by strips of molding, also the same color. And the mirror would match the bureau because it would match, and would be suspended by a gold cord with a decorative gold button concealing the hook and a gold tassel as the crowning effect. O beloved room, the steel girders structurally in place here overhead, neatly buried in their white cerements, giving Mr. Volente something to gaze upon while lying in bed; and the bathroom with the shower curtain on little roller hooks, a single shake being enough (O room!) to distribute the curtain the whole length of the tub, and the glass shelves of the medicine cabinet ready (and able) for the safekeeping of the brush, the cream, the paste, the things. In the closet would be the paper bag to catch the soiled clothes which if sent before eight would be returned on the afternoon of the third day. It was a biblical promise, the afternoon of the third day, almost.

New York lay stretched in midsummer languor under her trees in her thinnest dress, idly and beautifully to the eyes of Mr. Volente her lover. She lay this morning early in the arms of the heat, humorously and indulgently, as though, having bathed in night, she had emerged and not bothered to put anything on and had stretched out to let the air, what air there was, touch her along arms and legs and shoulders and forehead, he thought, admiringly. The trucks and the sudden acceleration and the flippant horn and the rustle of countless affairs somewhat retarded by the middle-of-summer pause in everything, these were the sounds of her normal breathing (if you knew her well enough and had lived with her at this season in the long past) and her pulse, normal. It was the hour the earliest people were entering the buildings. Awnings were being cranked down already to spread the agreeable shade, the rectangles of relief sketched on the sidewalks. In every street the glimpse he caught of some door or some vestibule or some window would stir his memory and call up the recollection of something in his life that had once been.

"It was in this doorway . . .

"It was down that side street . . .

"It was in the back room of this café that . . ."

That was the thing about New York, it was always bringing up something out of your past, something ridiculous or lovely or glistening. Here all round him, he mused, was unquestionably the closest written page in the book of his life; here in the city in the streets and alleys and behind the walls and in the booths and beneath the roofs and under the marquees and canopies were the scenes of the story he remembered in tranquillity, however poorly constructed, however unconvincing when retold.

In the short space of time it took the cab to go from Penn Station to the hotel Mr. Volente mentally made the long sentimental journey to the historical places of the past. He knew that in the flesh he would soon visit some of these spots, just in passing, when he got loose in the city—as he always did; the habit of revisitation was fixed in him, it was a date he kept with himself, unconsciously—the only date he regarded with complete seriousness in New York. It was always that way: when he got to town the first phone message he put through was to himself. Mr. Volente, calling Mr. Volente. Meanwhile, sitting in the cab, he piloted his thoughts swiftly to the ports they always called in. Here was Fifth Avenue and the Childs restaurant where the waitress had long ago spilled a bottle of buttermilk down his blue suit. A turning point, he liked to think. He often wondered where the girl was, this somehow invaluable and clumsy girl who had unwittingly shaped his life into a pattern from which it had not since departed. (Mr. Volente had written an account of the catastrophe at the time and had sold it to a young and inexperienced magazine, thus making for himself the enormously important discovery that the world would pay a man for setting down a simple, legible account of his own misfortunes. With the check in his pocket and trouble always at his elbow, the young Volente had faced life with fresh courage and had seen a long vista of profitable confession; and in fact he had stuck it out and done well enough.) I suppose I shall run out eventually, he thought dreamily, but I haven't yet. That poor girl—that waitress! Where is she? He should send her something, a large sum of money such as five dollars perhaps, or an autographed copy of his latest book, let's see, what was the name of it?

What is this we have here? A shop window. That's it. On University Place. It was while looking into this window that a small dog he had once loved (and a great window shopper) had been struck by a cab and killed. The very place. And the dog was a sort of symbol of something which was still alive, still very much alive, and must be kept forever safe against disaster and the badly driven cabs that there are in the world. University Place, corner of Eighth Street (careful about the car tracks that aren't there any more, Volente!), a stone's throw from the place—yes, there is the garden, visible through the iron gates, a comic pleasance surrounded by walls, the same pergolas, the same privet hedges, the brick paths, and the pinched and sooty symmetry. How infinitely refreshing it had seemed in those days and still seems now in memory, from the third-floor rear of the house where in the bedroom on the hot days the cool cross draft across the low rooftops of the Mews struck through, filtered of all devils by the coarse mesh of the fire escape, the peaceful ineradicable room! Farther west . . . it was in this block, it was here, in Washington Place, it was down these three steps, or is it four, in this now legitimate café once so lawless and hospitable, that they had dined the night they were married (only nobody knew) and had sipped the wine in joy. Here is the very lamppost (next block, please) under which, in another chapter, in another vein, with equal wonder and intensity . . .

This statue in the Square—something familiar here, Volente! Of course! Subject of a sonnet. Sonnet twenty-nine, the one with the tired feet. Yet how tender and fine and wonderful it had seemed on the occasion of its troubled birth!

It was here on this stoop he had vomited, but we will not dwell on that. He was always vomiting, thought Volente with a sigh. Nausea and love, the twin convulsions, one of the stomach, the other of the entire system sometimes called the heart. O passionate and disturbing city to whose innumerable small rooms, at whose uncountable tables he had committed the immediate problems of the soul, to have them clarified in the wine at evening and returned to him (as though by special messenger) on a tray the following morning—all those crazy little places, enno-bled by the so many confidences. (In those days, he thought, there was no air conditioning; the same air remained in the small rooms and moved about, distributed by a fan, from table to table with the drifting smoke, until the whole place gathered over a period of months and years an accumulation of ardor and love and adventure and hope, a fine natural patina on floors and walls, as a church accumulates piety and sorrow and holiness.)

Mr. Volente's cab moved swiftly but not so swiftly as his mind, which was in West Thirteenth Street in a remoter past, only the El was there and the shoeshine hat-cleaning parlor on the corner. It was up two flights, he thought, and heard the clicking of the release latch on the outer door and saw the polished plates of the letter boxes and read the names. Two flights up, what lean and tortured years, with those other fellows—all gainfully employed except himself—those mornings alone in the apartment straightening up after the others had left for work, rinsing the dirty cereal-encrusted bowls, taking the percolator apart and putting it together again, and then sinking down on the lumpy old couch in the terrible loneliness of midmorning, sometimes giving way to tears of doubt and misgiving (his own salt rivers of doubt), and in the back room the compensatory window box with the brave and grimy seedlings struggling, and the view of the naked fat lady across the yard. It had always been a question then of how to get through the day, the innumera-ble aimless journeys to remote sections of the town, inspecting ware-houses, docks, marshes, lumberyards, the interminable quest for the holy and unnameable grail, looking for it down every street and in every window and in every pair of eyes, following a star always obscured by mists. But there were also the noons in the restaurant in Waverly Place (it was through that door) studying the menu to get the biggest value for fifty cents including tip, studying the faces of the other lunchers and the answering grave look in the eyes of the girls and the constant and abiding riddle, and on fine warm June days in the back garden, the same food and ritual, in the ailanthus shade. And the healing night (Mr. Volente had glided swiftly down Sixth, turned right on West Fourth, then left on Barrow and vanished down a rabbit hole where he was welcomed by an Italian, and there would be the same cheap table d'hôte that he liked and the same girl with him that he loved, together discovering the indispens-able privacy of a dim and crowded room).

It was in this flower shop that I bought the . . . it was in the third booth from the door in the second restaurant from the corner that B. told me that . . . it was at this newsstand that I bought the Morning *World* that contained . . . here walked I under these great trees alone with my misery . . . it was from this drugstore that I phoned M. . . . it was up that narrow and deplorable stairway I ascended. . . .

Mr. Volente's mind skipped again, downtown to a doorway in Park Row. It was late Saturday afternoon in the fall of the year and he was standing in the lobby slowly eating Tokay grapes and spitting out the seeds. He had just quit his first job in New York and he was moodily eating the grapes by way of celebrating, in one inclusive ritual, the failure of his first major maneuver in life and the renewal of his liberty. His inability to cope with the requirements of the job was a stone in his stomach, to which he was now adding ripe grapes; but the sense that his movements were no longer circumscribed by the hands of a clock, the sense of the return of footlooseness, the sense of again being a reporter receiving only the vaguest and most mysterious assignments, was oxygen in his lungs. He stood there a long time, having nowhere in particular to go any more. An important doorway, he had always thought. He had never eaten a red grape since without tasting again the sweet tonic of rededication.

Ah, me, thought Mr. Volente.

Doorways! Had he never been anywhere except in some doorway for God's sake? There was an almost furtive quality to his past. Fourth Avenue in the Twenties, what are you doing here, Volente, in this doorway in this dreary section of Fourth Avenue? You know well enough—you know you are waiting, because you think if you wait cleverly enough, you will catch a glimpse of her as she gets out at five o'clock from her job in that woolen place unless it was a cotton place, anyway a glimpse being the only nourishment that this bitter day affords, and this waiting, like a hungry dog for a crust. I said hungry, Volente.

Gramercy is round the corner, the green Gramercy with the snobbish fence behind which the rich children ride the velocipedes from Schwarz's. It was in that park, keyless though I was at the time, said Mr. Volente . . .

Here is the house where I awoke after the ball was over and in the solemn dreadful noon put on the dinner jacket again, and the rumpled-bosomed formal shirt again, and traveled across town pretending I was a waiter or a musician on his way to keep an engagement. Here is the tower where my son was born, and the sound of the Sunday bells, and the angel of death in a starched uniform and the blood running slowly through the transfusing tubes.

The cab stopped at the Hotel of the Total Stranger, and Volente registered and was shown to his room, Number 704, the one with the mirror with the gold tassel. He unpacked, putting his razor and things in the medicine cabinet. After breakfast he walked out as he had known he would, and met the heat as he emerged into the street, and took the city in his arms affectionately and held her, with love and recognition. The people were moving slowly, the delivery boys in shirtsleeves with the half-moon of sweat under the armpit, the porter languidly shining the bronze standpipe with the creamy stuff from the old gin bottle, the cop in shirtsleeves, even his revolver wilting under the terrible blow from the sun. Mr. Volente strolled aimlessly over to Park Avenue and turned uptown. Presently he noticed a doorway that seemed familiar. He glanced at the number, then at the names on the plaque. Names of medical men. Volente smiled. It was in this building, on a May morning . . .

Volente sighed. O inscrutable and lovely town! O citadel of love.

FROM AN OFFICE

The smoke that follows noontime
    Rides down the rifts of walls;
Dirt and sun in the alley,
    Glimmering dust falls.

I hear the clack of the tickers,
    I tend the click of wires:
And dream of old leaves in gutters,
    And October fires.

READING ROOM

Sadness and languor along the oak tables
Steady the minds of the sitters and readers;
Sleep and despair, and the stealth of hunters,
And (in the man at the end of the row) anger.

Books are the door of escape from the forest,
Books are the wilderness, too, for the scholar;
Walled in the past, drowning in fables,
Out of the weather we sit, steady in languor.

Which are the ones that belong, properly?
Which are the hunters, which the harried?
Break not the hush that surrounds this miracle—
Mind against mind, coupling in splendor—
Step on no twig, disturbing the forest.
Enter the aisles of despair. Sit down and be quiet.

THE LADY IS COLD

(Intimations at Fifty-eighth Street)

The fountain is dry at the Plaza,
    The sycamore trees go bare;
The ivy is sere and it has a
    Resigned and immutable air.

The lady is cold at the fountain,
    The sitter is cold on the ledge,
The Plaza is gaunt as a mountain,
    The air is a knife with an edge.

But what is this sniff and this twitter,
    And what is the pluck at my vest?
What gleam in the eye of the sitter?
    What lamb of a cloud in the west?

The earth is but held in solution,
    And March will release before long
The lady in brazen ablution,
    The trees and the fountain in song!

PIGEON, SING CUCCU!

Earth is a hoyden, loud rejoice;
    Pigeon, sing cuccu!
The green girl, spring, has found her voice,
    My heart is piercèd through.

The warm wind picketh winter's locks,
    The jonquil bares his blade;
In Finley Shepard's window box
    The hyacinths parade.

From choir loft, in heavenly chants,
    Up swell the sweet hosannas.
The huckster fills his cart with plants
    Who lately called bananas.

By Rockefeller's skating pond,
    The cherry springeth clear,
And waveth wide the greenhouse frond
    And drops the pinking tear.

Love is alive beneath the pave,
    A-pipping at the shell;
Who has the fun that I have,
    Or loveth spring so well?

In glaumy glades and rocky rifts
    The snake from his cool slumber
Stirs, when the air of heaven sifts
    Into his noisome chamber.

Beside the Fifty-ninth Street lake
    Old men, alive and toothless,
Applaud the plundering of the drake
    And grin when love is ruthless.

Oh, swiftly floweth now the Bronx
    Where osier stem doth redden,
The sky is loud when the goose honks,
    And naught can my heart sadden.

Earth is a hoyden, loud rejoice;
    Pigeon, sing cuccu!
The green girl, spring, has made her choice,
    My heart is piercèd through.

SOLILOQUY AT TIMES SQUARE

The time for little words is past;
We now speak only the broad impertinences.
I take your hand
Merely to help you cross the street
(We are such friends),
Choosing the long and formal phrase
Deliberately.
At dinner we discuss, rather intelligently,
The things one should discuss at dinner. So.
How well we are in tune—how easy
Every phrase! The long words come, fondling the ear,
Flattering the mind they come. Long words
Enjoy the patronage of noble minds,
The circumspection of this sanity.

How much is gone! How much went
When the little words went: peace,
Sandwiched in the space between madness and madness;
The quick exchange of every bright moment;
The animal alertness to the other's heart;
The reality of nearness. Those things went
With the words.

Suppose I should forget, grow thoughtless—
What if the little words came back,
Running in upon me, running back
Like little children home from school?
Suppose I spoke—oh, I don't know—
Some vagrant phrase out of the summer!
What if I said: "I love you"? Something as simple
And as easy to the tongue as that—
Something as true? I'm only talking.
Give me your hand,
We must by all means cross this street.

VILLAGE REVISITED

(A cheerful lament in which truth, pain, and beauty are
prominently mentioned, and in that order)

In the days of my youth, in the days of my youth,
I lay in West Twelfth Street, writhing with Truth.
I died in Jones Street, dallying with pain,
And flashed up Sixth Avenue, risen again.

In the terrible beautiful age of my prime,
I lacked for sweet linen but never for time.
The tree in the alley was potted in gold,
The girls on the buses would never grow old.

Last night with my love I returned to these haunts
To visit Pain's diggings and try for Truth's glance;
I was eager and ardent and waited as always
The answering click to my ring in the hallways,
But Truth hardly knew me, and Pain wasn't in
(It scarcely seemed possible Pain wasn't in).

Beauty recalled me. We bowed in the Square,
In the wonderful westerly Waverly air.
She had a new do, I observed, to her hair.

SPRINGTIME CROSSTOWN EPISODE IN FOUR-TIME

As I was crossing Chatham Bar
    In Forty-which Street west of Lex,
An Eastern Doorman sprang from cover,
    Unmistakable as to sex:
A brilliant Doorman, adult male,
With flashpatch wings and rufous tail,
A piping Doorman whistling clear,
And oh, it was a song to hear!
    Chwee . . . whee,
    And a skyview taxi-taxi-taxi.

The morn was tied with Aprilstrings,
    The bar was warm, the air was sweet,
The Doorman danced and drooped his wings
    And circled bravely in the street.
And when his whistling drew no cab,
Out from the tangle, shy and drab,
A female crept—a little doxy,
Drawn more sure than any taxi.

The Eastern Doorman quit his questing,
Chirruped twice, and they went to nesting.
    Chwee . . . whee!

SPAIN IN FIFTY-NINTH STREET

Seated in one of the Spanish chairs,
In the Spanish Childs, was a man of affairs.
From his russet shoes to his silk cravat,
He was a man worth looking at.
His pointed toes and his rounded middle,
His costly food from the Spanish griddle,
Were marks of a man who had learned to live,
In every sense an Executive.

Wandering chaste through the Spanish aisle,
There came a hostess, free from guile.
With her noble step and her menu pendent,
She was the perfect Childs attendant.
She was the girl, should you need more butter,
Primed with a sense of service utter.
With her wavy hair and her lack of fat,
She was a girl worth looking at.

"How do you do?" said the man of affairs.
"How do you do?" said the hostess.

That was the whole extent of their meeting;
That was the long and short of their greeting.
But I noted the pause in the act of swallowing,
And the eyes in the wake of the hostess following.
And I saw, in the Spanish sunlight dancing,
The modest smile in the backward glancing,
Quick as the passing of summer rain,
Bright as the streets of a town in Spain.

"How do you do?" thought the man of affairs.
"How do you *do?*" thought the hostess.

A TABLE FOR ONE

In a medium-priced restaurant where I go to die,
There is this little bob-tailed fly.

Let me order the filet of sole meunière,
Swishing his buckle he will be there
To buzz the fish
And deflower the dish.

Or say I start with the onion soup:
He makes it his boast
That he can beat me to the partially submerged toast.
If I should get there first with a sprinkle of Parmesan,
He quickly possesses the cheese
On his hands and knees,
This little bob-tailed kid.

Suppose I sit late, lingering over the peach in wine,
I will hear his engines,
Watch the wingover, the approach, the swift incline,
Then, what is technically mine
Becomes his, and he likes it fine.

I do not know how he lost part of his tail—
In some flare-up in the kitchen I have no doubt,
Slashed in the act of coupling with his frail
By a mad waiter whose patience had run out.
All I know for sure is that my "table for one,"
Being within his reach,
Is a mere figure of speech.

TWINS

On a warm, miserable morning last week I went up to the Bronx Zoo to see the moose calf and to break in a new pair of black shoes. I encountered better luck than I had bargained for. The cow moose and her young one were standing near the wall of the deer park below the monkey house, and in order to get a better view I strolled down to the lower end of the park, by the brook. The path there is not much traveled. As I approached the corner where the brook trickles under the wire fence, I noticed a red deer getting to her feet. Beside her, on legs that were just learning their business, was a spotted fawn, as small and perfect as a trinket seen through a reducing glass. They stood there, mother and child, under a gray beech whose trunk was engraved with dozens of hearts and initials. Stretched on the ground was another fawn, and I realized that the doe had just finished twinning. The second fawn was still wet, still unrisen. Here was a scene of rare sylvan splendor, in one of my five favorite boroughs, and I couldn't have asked for more. Even my new shoes seemed to be working out all right and weren't hurting much.

The doe was only a couple of feet from the wire, and I sat down on a rock at the edge of the footpath to see what sort of start young fawns get in the deep fastnesses of Mittel Bronx. The mother, mildly resentful of my presence and dazed from her labor, raised one forefoot and stamped primly. Then she lowered her head, picked up the afterbirth, and began dutifully to eat it, allowing it to swing crazily from her mouth, as though it were a bunch of withered beet greens. From the monkey house came the loud, insane hooting of some captious primate, filling the whole woodland with a wild hooroar. As I watched, the sun broke weakly through, brightened the rich red of the fawns, and kindled their white spots. Occasionally a sightseer would appear and wander aimlessly by, but of all who passed none was aware that anything extraordinary had occurred. "Looka the kangaroos!" a child cried. And he and his mother stared sullenly at the deer and then walked on.

In a few moments the second twin gathered all his legs and all his ingenuity and arose, to stand for the first time sniffing the mysteries of a park for captive deer. The doe, in recognition of his achievement, quit her other work and began to dry him, running her tongue against the grain and paying particular attention to the key points. Meanwhile the first fawn tiptoed toward the shallow brook, in little stops and goes, and started across. He paused midstream to make a slight contribution, as a child does in bathing. Then, while his mother watched, he continued across, gained the other side, selected a hiding place, and lay down under a skunk-cabbage leaf next to the fence, in perfect concealment, his legs folded neatly under him. Without actually going out of sight, he had managed to disappear completely in the shifting light and shade. From somewhere a long way off a twelve-o'clock whistle sounded. I hung around awhile, but he never budged. Before I left, I crossed the brook myself, just outside the fence, knelt, reached through the wire, and tested the truth of what I had once heard: that you can scratch a new fawn between the ears without starting him. You can indeed.

THE ROCK DOVE

I wonder if anyone has ever seen a baby pigeon in New York City? Or are they hatched fully grown? . . . I wonder if the pigeons in midtown Manhattan drink water, and, if so, where do they find it? . . . I wonder where pigeons have their nests, or don't they? . . . I wonder why pigeons live in cities? . . . I wonder why pigeons are so fond of air conditioners? But, pigeons, thank you for making my life so full of wonder. Or is it Manhattan, *en toto,* that does it?

—EUGENIA BEDELL in *Promenade*

It has never been my desire to diminish by so much as a crumb of information the charming wonderment of a lady. Yet the above questions have been asked publicly. They stand plain and inquiring, crying for direct answers. I shall take them up in the order of their appearance.

Q: I wonder if anyone has ever seen a baby pigeon in New York City?

A: Yes, cases have been reported. I saw a squab this afternoon in a nest at No. 813 Fifth Avenue, third floor front, a short walk from the men's bar of Carlton House, one of the hotels that sponsor *Promenade.* The nest commands a view of the pony ride in Central Park, enjoys a fashionable address, and belongs to the baroque school of pigeons' nests (Fig. I).

Q: Are they hatched fully grown?

A: When hatched, a squab is about the size of a pigeon's egg. Except for patches of fuzz, it is as naked as a baby. It attains full stature in about four weeks, during which time the parent birds will probably have started a second nest. Pigeons, being city dwellers by choice, have caught the excitement of New York, and, like an executive who enjoys having two phones on his desk, a pair of pigeons like to keep two nests going at the same time. They deliberately place themselves under this sort of pressure.The pair at 813 Fifth Avenue, as I write, have two nests, both at that address. Squabs are being fed in one, eggs are being incubated in the other (Fig. I). Busy days! The cock and the hen take turns sitting on the eggs and pumping pigeon's milk into the mouths of the young. Pigeon's milk is a regurgitated substance. It is made of popcorn and ice and all things nice.

Q: I wonder if the pigeons in midtown Manhattan drink water, and, if so, where do they find it?

A: Pigeons in all five boroughs drink water. They drink it not as a fowl does, by scooping a few drops up and letting them trickle down its throat, but as a child does when it sucks a soda through a straw. On wet days, pigeons find water everywhere—in gutters, depressions in the sidewalk, discarded containers. In dry spells, pigeons hunt about for water. A truck draws up to deliver shaved ice to a restaurant, a few flakes of ice fall to the pavement; pigeons swoop down to await the tiny thaw. In freezing weather, pigeons seek subway ventilators and other flues, where the warm draft creates local melting conditions. A thirsty pigeon will drink almost any sort of Manhattan cocktail: the creamy spillage from a caterer's tray blended with the drip from the tailpipe of a cross-town bus. I have watched a thirsty pigeon sip sidewalk juices that would turn the stomach of a hog. In a pinch, a pigeon can fly to the yak's yard in the zoo and drink from the fountain.

Fig. 1. Baroque

Q: I wonder where pigeons have their nests?

A: At this writing, pigeons have their nests at 18 East Fiftieth Street (Engel Furs); at 42 West Forty-fourth Street (Bar Association); at the freight entrance to 444 Madison Avenue; atop one of the trefoils of a gable in the Lady Chapel of St. Patrick's Cathedral, between Fiftieth and Fifty-first; on a window ledge in the south face of St. Thomas's, on Fifty-third just west of Fifth; under an air conditioner at 912 Fifth Avenue; on a ledge at 867 Madison Avenue, above Jean Beecher Sample Hats; in an embrasure of the Seventh Regiment Armory, about twelve feet west of Lexington Avenue; at 64 East Sixty-sixth Street, on a capital near a bowed window with stained-glass panes; and at 901 Fifth Avenue, just north of Frick's flowering magnolias. Other addresses of pigeons can be obtained by watching pigeons. I have listed only those I happen to be aware of at the moment.

Nests change from day to day. Pigeons are fast workers. Nests usually contain only two eggs and the eggs hatch in seventeen days. Squabs develop with amazing rapidity. By the time these answers to Miss Bedell's questions appear, the whole scene will have changed, for better or for worse: nests that now contain eggs will contain young birds; nests that now contain young birds will be inactive, the squabs having flown or been pushed out of the nest to join the great crew of city pigeons.

I have illustrated four common types of nests: the baroque, the modern, the Gothic, and the military. There are many others. The hen at 912 Fifth Avenue (Fig. II) has gone modern but is paying a heavy price. The air conditioner gives her a broad, protecting roof, but there is insufficient headroom. She must crouch for seventeen days. Furthermore, there is almost no room for nesting material. From my vantage point across the

Avenue, it appeared that the bird was forced to lay her eggs on the bare ledge, where they are in danger of rolling off. I was unable to use my binoculars on this nest, not wanting to risk arrest, so my report is not as reliable as I would wish.

Fig. II. Modern

The nest on the trefoil of the Lady Chapel (Fig. III) is one of several Gothic nests in that vicinity. The bird in this nest has an unobstructed view into Bennett Cerf's office in Random House. She can sit by the hour watching the publisher make his hard decisions preparatory to appearing on "What's My Line?," where all he has to do is guess that the contestant sells inner soles in the Outer Hebrides. Publishers lead lives as varied and shameless as pigeons, but are less beautiful against the sky.

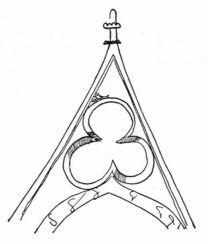

Fig. III. Gothic

The bird in Figure IV (military) has built an unusually ambitious nest for a pigeon. This bird is large and in fine plumage; the nest is well conceived, well executed. The Seventh Regiment Armory is in great demand by nesting birds. Every available embrasure is either occupied or being fought over. A few of the embrasures, however, have been fitted with pigeon baffles by the military. Here again I was handicapped by city conditions; when I found myself standing in front of the Cosmopolitan Club, on Sixty-sixth Street, peering at the Seventh Regiment Armory through binoculars, I felt as though I were taking snapshots of Fort Knox. I put the glasses away immediately and did not see as much as I wished.

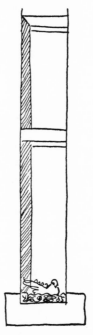

Fig. IV. Military

Q: I wonder why pigeons live in cities?

A: The city pigeon is a descendant of the wild rock dove, a bird of cliffs and ledges. Pigeons live in cities because a city offers cliffs and ledges. Unlike the robin and the barn swallow, the rock dove, or "pigeon," has no natural talent for nest-building. What a pigeon needs is just what the city provides in abundance: a nook, a ledge, a recess, a niche, a capital, an outcropping, the tin elbow of a downspout, the bronze musette bag of a war hero, the concrete beard of a saint, the narrow channel between two buildings. (A good example of the channel nest is the one at the freight entrance of 444 Madison, around the corner on Fiftieth.) In April, when airs are soft, the very sight of a slot, a scroll, a squinch, a corbiestep, a buttress, a transom, a ventilator, is enough to send the cockbird whirling in circles and set his neck feathers on fire. The hen, equally excited but less willing to admit it, finally drops her defenses and picks up a few twigs. Besides offering a pigeon a wide choice of home sites, the city gives a pigeon a free lunch, and pigeons have taken up with men for much the same reason cowbirds have taken up with cows—there's a living in it. Unfortunately, the diet of city pigeons is too salty (handouts of salted nuts), and many birds suffer from salt poisoning.

Pigeons' nests are everywhere at this happy season. They go largely unobserved, however. Most nests are more than five feet above the ground (pigeons prefer second- and third-floor locations), and New Yorkers do not ordinarily lift their gaze above eye level. While studying the nest shown in Figure IV, I stood across the street from the Armory and watched the passersby. The pigeon sat only about fifteen feet above the sidewalk, yet hundreds of people walked by without seeing the fine spectacle of a bird on eggs in springtime. Most of those who passed seemed deep in thought—scheming, worrying, hoping, dreaming, but not looking, or at any rate not looking *up*. The location of a pigeon's nest is often betrayed by the parent that is off duty at the moment. When you see a pigeon standing perfectly still and looking bored, scan the nearby ledges and you will usually discover the mate, quiet on the eggs.

Q: I wonder why pigeons are so fond of air conditioners?

A: Air conditioners form nooks with window casings (Fig. II).

Q: But, pigeons, thank you for making my life so full of wonder. Or is it Manhattan, *en toto,* that does it?

A: I am hampered in answering this question by not knowing the meaning of *"en toto."* The phrase does not turn up in my reference books. I knew a gorilla once named M'Toto, and there is a barroom in the John Ringling Hotel, in Sarasota, Florida, called the M'Toto Room, but *"en toto"* is another matter. As for the wellsprings of wonderment, they run deep. The quiet mind, the youthful heart, the perceptive eye, the racing blood—these conflow to produce wonder. Manhattan Island, entire, can sometimes cause such a confluence. For me, the nesting bird can cause it every time.

Because of the trend toward plainer façades, the city of the future may hold no charm for pigeons. Lever House offers little inducement to a nesting pair. As far as that goes, unless men cultivate the dove more successfully than they appear to be doing in this century, the city of the future may be inhospitable to men and doves alike. (The pigeon, strange to say, is closely related to the dodo.) But there are still doves among us.

While they endure we must note their locations, elevate our gaze above the level of our immediate concerns, imbibe the sweet air and perfect promise: the egg miraculous upon the ledge, the bird compact upon the egg, its generous warmth, its enviable patience, its natural fortitude and grace.

BUSINESS SHOW

It was a soft afternoon with smoke rising in straws of light from the chimneys, and pink clouds the color of chrysanthemums folded gently against a pale sky. Even Eighth Avenue seemed to dwell in heavenly pallor when I left it to plunge into the Business Show and walk in the chattering aisles of calculators, addressographs, electric tabulation machines, where girls in purest white satin, enthroned on chromium chairs, their blond hair gleaming like clouds, their nails shining pink the color of chrysanthemums, pushed the little shining keys—tick, tap, PULL, tick, tap, PULL—adding, subtracting, filing, assembling, addressing, dictaphoning, typing, silhouetted firmly against the pure walls of steel that was grained to look like wood, and the murmurous mysteries of business enlarged a hundred times, staggering the mind. Adoringly I paused before each machine, as a traveler before a shrine; and it all seemed more mechanistic than any play I had ever seen, even than the plays produced by the little groups who take the theater seriously. But what I noticed was that the seeming dominance of the machines was an illusion of the senses, that the electric current was in fact impotent, for everywhere I saw men standing gravely talking to the girls in purest white satin, and always something passed between them, something a little extra in their look, the eyes of the girls returning the clear, desirous gaze of the builders of the incredible machines, giving back desire for desire, and that the current of this exchange (the exciting unfulfillment) was the thing in all the room, and not the chattering mysteries of the addition, tabulation, punctuation, subtraction, which were as nothing, which were as an accompaniment (tick, tap, PULL) to the loud, insistent, throbbing song of beauty unattainable, hair (like clouds) infinitely desirable (in a hall on Eighth Avenue), with smoke rising in straws of light from the chimneys.

RAINMAKERS

When he was told that people were bringing suit against the makers of rain, Mayor O'Dwyer, the rainmaker, said, "Somebody doesn't want it to rain, I take it." This remark belongs right up with the more cocky utterances of self-reliant man, alongside Hague's famous pronouncement: "I am the law." It was almost as though the Mayor had said, "I am the rain." By putting in their place those who took an opposite view of rain, he reduced precipitation to simple dogma. His was not a demagogic remark, like Hague's—simply an Olympian remark, innocent and infinitely remote. Somebody indeed doesn't want it to rain—some almost, but not quite, forgotten man. How about this fellow? He interests us. Crotchety, probably. Or maybe an inveterate picnicker. But a man, nevertheless—two arms, two legs, an umbrella, and a habit of looking to the limitless sky for his rewards and punishments, not to a city father.

An arresting quality in modern man is his attitude toward his natural surroundings, a quality likely to get him in trouble and even shorten his stay on earth. He commonly thinks of himself as having been here since the beginning—older than the crab—and he also likes to think he's destined to stay to the bitter end. Actually, he is a late comer, and there are moments when he shows every sign of being an early leaver—a patron who bows out after a few gaudy and memorable scenes. It is entirely in keeping with man's feeling about nature that when he suddenly notices his drinking fountain losing pressure, he should ascend to heaven and beat a cloud over the ears. Petulance, coupled with insatiable curiosity, and the will to dominate. "Somebody doesn't want it to rain, I take it," said the Mayor, while the lightning played all around his words.

The city presumably feels it has a pretty good legal loophole. Even if a plane goes up and seeds a cloud, and rain falls, the wet people down below will have to prove that the seed germinated, that the rain was in fact the fruit of the seed. This may be hard to prove. Legally, rainmaking may be in the clear as a device. Philosophically, rainmaking is anything but in the clear—it is in a misty mid-region. There is more to rain than meets the kitchen tap of a city dweller; rain is part of the stuff of melancholia, part of darkness, of husbandry, of sport, and of retailing. Everyone talks about the weather because the weather is every man's chattel. The suicide often holds off until it rains, and the pilot who seeds a cloud may be seeding a man, too, and causing the ultimate and unbearable teardrop. The rain pilot's flight is a long, long flight—into the wild gray yonder.

New York's water shortage is caused less by lack of rain than by lack of foresight, lack of a decent feeling for nature. The remedy, it seems to me, is not the manufacture of rain but the correct use and distribution of whatever rain naturally arrives on earth. If, as the rainmakers would have it, man does invade the sky and nudge clouds, his flight will, I predict, be but the beginning of such practices, and we shall find the makers of lightning also aloft, to satisfy the desires of the manufacturers of lightning rods, who may decide that lightning is in short supply and devise a way of setting more of it loose. This, in turn, will be an affront to insurance companies, who must stand the cost of retopping chimneys that get hit by the bolts. In short, it is conceivable that man may have to set an arbitrary limit to his domain—draw a line where he ends and God begins. The Mayor may think he is the rain, but when he pours he may have a surprise coming.

THE TWENTIETH CENTURY
GETS THROUGH

The Twentieth Century Limited, First Time It Has Reached
City This Winter Covered with Icicles. It Forged Its Way
Through the Blizzards Upstate and in the West. Mae Murray
Is Pictured Standing Beside the Train.
> —Caption of photograph in *The World*

The storm king whistled from out the North
As the crack old Limited train set forth,
    With a hey nonny nonny.

The snow blew strong through the long, long night,
And settled on objects left and right,
But the Twentieth Century plowed on through
As a limited train is supposed to do,
With Buffalo, Syracuse, Canastota,
Beneath more snow than their usual quota,
    And a hey nonny nonny.

From the chilly blast and the raging gale,
The Century gathered a coat of mail,
And through the blizzard it plunged and reared
With ice for whiskers, snow for a beard,
Through miles of sleet and hours of snowing
There was one bright thought that kept it going:
"If I get to New York in a great big hurry
"They'll take my picture with sweet Mae Murray,
    "With a hey nonny nonny,
    "And a mae murray murray."

That was the trend of the Century's thought
As on through the fearful night it fought:
"I couldn't keep on through the Mohawk Valley
"For Lillian Gish or Marion Talley,
"But a blizzard to me is the veriest flurry
"If it leads to a photo with Mistress Murray,
    "With a mae murray murray."

So the Century train, with a sob and a shiver,
Continued its course down the Hudson River,

And weary from battling in storm and stress,
Pulled in and was met by the daily press,
And there, sure enough, looking warm and furry,
Was the dear little figure of Mistress Murray
Who, laying a hand on the Century's ice,
Appeared in all papers in less than a trice.
    With a mae murray murray.

Now here is a thing that I'm anxious to know
In the matter of pictures of ice and snow:
Assuming that turnabout *is* fair play,
Would photographs work in the opposite way?
Suppose Mae Murray came out of the West
With snow in her hair and ice on her chest,
With frost on her eyelid, sleet on her nose,
Could she make the Twentieth Century pose?
Would they take a picture of just those two,
Miss Murray's face all chapped and blue?
With the caption: "Girl Comes Grimly Through"?

Would the New York Central be quick to send
The cream of its trains to the side of a friend
Arriving in town all cold and shaken
And ready to have her picture taken?
    With a hey nonny nonny?

And unless they would, which I gravely doubt,
Why, what are these pictures all about?
    With a mae murray murray?

BOSTON IS LIKE NO OTHER PLACE
IN THE WORLD ONLY MORE SO

When I am out of funds and sorts
    And life is all in snarls,
I quit New York and travel east
    To Boston on the Charles.

In Boston, life is smoother far,
    It's easier and freer,
Where every boy's a Harvard man
    And every man's a skier.

And there I know a small hotel
    Whose rates are not too high,
Alive with ancient Boston dames
    Who have refused to die.

A lobby full of stately palms,
    A chef that's quite insane,
Martinis yellow as the rose
    And warm as summer rain.

There's something in the Boston scene
    So innocent, so tranquil,
It takes and holds my interest
    The same as any bank will.

For Boston's not a capital,
    And Boston's not a place;
Rather I think that Boston is
    A sort of state of grace.

The people's lives in Boston
    Are flowers blown in glass;
On Commonwealth, on Beacon,
    They bow and speak and pass.

No man grows old in Boston,
    No lady ever dies;
No youth is ever wicked,
    No infant ever cries.

No orthodox Bostonian
    Is lonely or dejected,
For everyone in Boston
    With everyone's connected.

So intricate the pattern,
    The barroom of the Ritz
Becomes a jigsaw puzzle,
    Each life a piece that fits.

At symphonies and weddings
    The young debs spend their days;
They glide through cocktail lounges
    Carrying huge bouquets.

Each Boston girl is swept along
    Down the predestined channel
To where she meets a Boston boy
    Alert in Brooksian flannel,

Magnificent in fallen socks,
    His hair like stubble weeds,
His elbow patch an earnest of
    The fellowship of tweeds.

When Muzak plays in Boston,
    It wakes celestial strings,
And I can sit in Boston
    And think of many things,

For Boston's not a capital,
    And Boston's not a place;
Rather I feel that Boston is
    The perfect state of grace.

After a week of Boston
    I rise and take the train,
And I am always very glad
    To see New York again.

New York seems doubly beautiful,
    Its air as clear as Heaven's;
New York—where life is always
    At sixes and at sevens,

Where no one ever marries right,
    And girls go off their trolley,
And young men go to N.Y.U.,
    To Fordham, and to Poly,

Where hackmen have peculiar names
    And relatives afar,
And one can watch the Chrysler spire
    Bisect the morning star.

I PAINT WHAT I SEE

*(A Ballad of Artistic Integrity, on the Occasion
of the Removal of Some Rather Expensive Murals
from the RCA Building in the Year 1933)*

"What do you paint, when you paint on a wall?"
    Said John D.'s grandson Nelson.
"Do you paint just anything there at all?
"Will there be any doves, or a tree in fall?
"Or a hunting scene, like an English hall?"

    "I paint what I see," said Rivera.

"What are the colors you use when you paint?"
    Said John D.'s grandson Nelson.
"Do you use any red in the beard of a saint?
"If you do, is it terribly red, or faint?
"Do you use any blue? Is it Prussian?"

    "I paint what I paint," said Rivera.

"Whose is that head that I see on my wall?"
    Said John D.'s grandson Nelson.
"Is it anyone's head whom we know, at all?
"A Rensselaer, or a Saltonstall?
"Is it Franklin D.? Is it Mordaunt Hall?
"Or is it the head of a Russian?"

    "I paint what I think," said Rivera.

    "I paint what I paint, I paint what I see,
    "I paint what I think," said Rivera,
    "And the thing that is dearest in life to me
    "In a bourgeois hall is Integrity;
    "However . . .
    "I'll take out a couple of people drinkin'
    "And put in a picture of Abraham Lincoln;
    "I could even give you McCormick's reaper
    "And still not make my art much cheaper.
    "But the head of Lenin has got to stay
    "Or my friends will give me the bird today,
    "The bird, the bird, forever."

"It's not good taste in a man like me,"
    Said John D.'s grandson Nelson,

"To question an artist's integrity
"Or mention a practical thing like a fee,
"But I know what I like to a large degree,
    "Though art I hate to hamper;
"For twenty-one thousand conservative bucks
"You painted a radical. I say shucks,
    "I never could rent the offices—
    "The capitalistic offices.
"For this, as you know, is a public hall
"And people want doves, or a tree in fall,
"And though your art I dislike to hamper,
"I owe a *little* to God and Gramper,
    "And after all,
    "It's *my* wall . . ."

    "We'll see if it is," said Rivera.

THE DOOR

Everything (he kept saying) is something it isn't. And everybody is always somewhere else. Maybe it was the city, being in the city, that made him feel how queer everything was and that it was something else. Maybe (he kept thinking) it was the names of the things. The names were tex and frequently koid. Or they were flex and oid or they were duroid (sani) or flexsan (duro), but everything was glass (but not quite glass) and the thing that you touched (the surface, washable, crease-resistant) was rubber, only it wasn't quite rubber and you didn't quite touch it but almost. The wall, which was glass but thrutex, turned out on being approached not to be a wall, it was something else, it was an opening or doorway—and the doorway (through which he saw himself approaching) turned out to be something else, it was a wall. And what he had eaten not having agreed with him.

He was in a washable house, but he wasn't sure. Now about those rats, he kept saying to himself. He meant the rats that the Professor had driven crazy by forcing them to deal with problems which were beyond the scope of rats, the insoluble problems. He meant the rats that had been trained to jump at the square card with the circle in the middle, and the card (because it was something it wasn't) would give way and let the rat into a place where the food was, but then one day it would be a trick played on the rat, and the card would be changed, and the rat would jump but the card wouldn't give way, and it was an impossible situation (for a rat) and the rat would go insane and into its eyes would come the unspeakably bright imploring look of the frustrated, and after the convulsions were over and the frantic racing around, then the passive stage would set in and the willingness to let anything be done to it, even if it was something else.

He didn't know which door (or wall) or opening in the house to jump at, to get through, because one was an opening that wasn't a door (it was a void, or koid) and the other was a wall that wasn't an opening, it was a sanitary cupboard of the same color. He caught a glimpse of his eyes staring into his eyes, in the thrutex, and in them was the expression he had seen in the picture of the rats—weary after convulsions and the frantic racing around, when they were willing and did not mind having anything done to them. More and more (he kept saying) I am confronted by a problem which is incapable of solution (for this time even if he chose the right door, there would be no food behind it) and that is what madness is, and things seeming different from what they are. He heard, in the house where he was, in the city to which he had gone (as toward a door which might, or might not, give way), a noise—not a loud noise but more of a low prefabricated humming. It came from a place in the base of the wall (or stat) where the flue carrying the filterable air was, and not far from the Minipiano, which was made of the same material nail-brushes are made of, and which was under the stairs. "This, too, has been tested," she said, pointing, but not at it, "and found viable." It wasn't a loud noise, he kept thinking, sorry that he had seen his eyes, even though it was through his own eyes that he had seen them.

First will come the convulsions (he said), then the exhaustion, then the willingness to let anything be done. "And you better believe it *will* be."

All his life he had been confronted by situations which were incapable of being solved, and there was a deliberateness behind all this, behind this changing of the card (or door), because they would always wait till you had learned to jump at the certain card (or door)—the one with the circle—and then they would change it on you. There have been so many doors changed on me, he said, in the last twenty years, but it is now becoming clear that it is an impossible situation, and the question is whether to jump again, even though they ruffle you in the rump with a blast of air—to make you jump. He wished he wasn't standing by the Minipiano. First they would teach you the prayers and the Psalms, and that would be the right door (the one with the circle), and the long sweet words with the holy sound, and that would be the one to jump at to get where the food was. Then one day you jumped and it didn't give way, so that all you got was the bump on the nose, and the first bewilderment, the first young bewilderment.

I don't know whether to tell her about the door they substituted or not, he said, the one with the equation on it and the picture of the amoeba reproducing itself by division. Or the one with the photostatic copy of the check for thirty-two dollars and fifty cents. But the jumping was so long ago, although the bump is . . . how those old wounds hurt! Being crazy this way wouldn't be so bad if only, if only. If only when you put your foot forward to take a step, the ground wouldn't come up to meet your foot the way it does. And the same way in the street (only I may never get back to the street unless I jump at the right door), the curb coming up to meet your foot, anticipating ever so delicately the weight of the body, which is somewhere else. "We could take your name," she said, "and send it to you." And it wouldn't be so bad if only you could read a sentence all the way through without jumping (your eye) to something else on the same page; and then (he kept thinking) there was that man out in Jersey, the one who started to chop his trees down, one by one, the man who began talking about how he would take his house to pieces, brick by brick, because he faced a problem incapable of solution, probably, so he began to hack at the trees in the yard, began to pluck with trembling fingers at the bricks in the house. Even if a house is not washable, it is worth taking down. It is not till later that the exhaustion sets in.

But it is inevitable that they will keep changing the doors on you, he said, because that is what they are for; and the thing is to get used to it and not let it unsettle the mind. But that would mean not jumping, and you can't. Nobody can not jump. There will be no not-jumping. Among rats, perhaps, but among people never. Everybody has to keep jumping at a door (the one with the circle on it) because that is the way everybody is, specially some people. You wouldn't want me, standing here, to tell you, would you, about my friend the poet (deceased) who said, "My heart has followed all my days something I cannot name"? (It had the circle on it.) And like many poets, although few so beloved, he is gone. It killed him, the jumping. First, of course, there were the preliminary bouts, the convulsions, and the calm and the willingness.

I remember the door with the picture of the girl on it (only it was spring), her arms outstretched in loveliness, her dress (it was the one with the circle on it) uncaught, beginning the slow, clear, blinding cascade—and I guess we would all like to try that door again, for it seemed like the way and for a while it was the way, the door would open and you would go through winged and exalted (like any rat) and the food would be there, the way the Professor had it arranged, everything O.K., and you had chosen the right door for the world was young. The time they changed that door on me, my nose bled for a hundred hours—how do you like that, Madam? Or would you prefer to show me further through this so strange house, or you could take my name and send it to me, for although my heart has followed all my days something I cannot name, I am tired of the jumping and I do not know which way to go, Madam, and I am not even sure that I am not tried beyond the endurance of man (rat, if you will) and have taken leave of sanity. What are you following these days, old friend, after your recovery from the last bump? What is the name, or is it something you cannot name? The rats have a name for it by this time, perhaps, but I don't know what they call it. I call it plexikoid and it comes in sheets, something like insulating board, unattainable and ugli-proof.

And there was the man out in Jersey, because I keep thinking about his terrible necessity and the passion and trouble he had gone to all those years in the indescribable abundance of a householder's detail, building the estate and the planting of the trees and in spring the lawn dressing and in fall the bulbs for the spring burgeoning, and the watering of the grass on the long light evenings in summer and the gravel for the driveway (all had to be thought out, planned) and the decorative borders, probably, the perennials and the bug spray, and the building of the house from plans of the architect, first the sills, then the studs, then the full corn in the ear, the floors laid on the floor timbers, smoothed, and then the carpets upon the smooth floors and the curtains and the rods therefor. And then, almost without warning, he would be jumping at the same old door and it wouldn't give: they had changed it on him, making life no longer supportable under the elms in the elm shade, under the maples in the maple shade.

"Here you have the maximum of openness in a small room."

It was impossible to say (maybe it was the city) what made him feel the way he did, and I am not the only one either, he kept thinking—ask any doctor if I am. The doctors, they know how many there are, they even know where the trouble is only they don't like to tell you about the prefrontal lobe because that means making a hole in your skull and removing the work of centuries. It took so long coming, this lobe, so many, many years. (Is it something you read in the paper, perhaps?) And now, the strain being so great, the door having been changed by the Professor once too often . . . but it only means a whiff of ether, a few deft strokes, and the higher animal becomes a little easier in his mind and more like the lower one. From now on, you see, that's the way it will be, the ones with the small prefrontal lobes will win because the other ones are hurt too much by this incessant bumping. They can stand just so much, eh, Doctor? (And what is that, pray, that you have in your hand?) Still, you never can tell, eh, Madam?

He crossed (carefully) the room, the thick carpet under him softly, and went toward the door carefully, which was glass and he could see himself in it, and which, at his approach, opened to allow him to pass through; and beyond he half expected to find one of the old doors that he had known, perhaps the one with the circle, the one with the girl her arms outstretched in loveliness and beauty before him. But he saw instead a moving stairway, and descended in light (he kept thinking) to the street below and to the other people. As he stepped off, the ground came up slightly, to meet his foot.

II

DIVINE

INTUITIONS

OF POESY

H. L. MENCKEN MEETS A POET
IN THE WEST SIDE Y.M.C.A.

POET: Good morrow, sweet Mencken,
Sweet Mencken, good morrow.
This is the West Side Y.M.C.A.
We got asphodel, we got coconut oil.
Tell us about the three abominations, Mr. M.

MENCKEN (Picking the skin off a medicine ball):
Poetry, religion, and Franklin D.
The three abominations be.
Why mince words? I do not feel
Kindly toward the Nouveau Deal.
Hopkins peddles quack elixir,
Tugwell is a phony fixer.
    Another lapse
    For Homo saps.
Yahweh!
(He throws the medicine ball and it turns into a Methodist bishop.)

POET: Now there are three of us.
May I offer you a cigarette, Bishop?

BISHOP: What was that crack about religion?
I'm an evangel, pure and voluble.

MENCKEN: Things unsolved are still insoluble.
The church is just an anodyne;
So are Old Fashioneds and so is wine.
The world wants solace when it's grieved.
I drink beer, but I'm not deceived.
Alcohol is a glut in the larder
Except to induce connubial ardor.

POET: Are you talking about love?

MENCKEN: I'm talkin' 'bout devil crabs, son.

POET: Tell the Bishop about the three abominations. He probably
didn't hear when you got it off the other time.

MENCKEN *(Chanting):* Poetry, religion, and Franklin D.
The three abominations be.
When the world is out of kilter
Someone always brews a philter.
This time it is sunny Frank
Pulling rabbits from his hank.
Preacher, poet, seer, and quack
Simply set the people back.
Stuff like Marx's rumble-bumble
Always makes the ninnies tumble.
Thorstein Veblen dished peruna,
Henry George was goona goona.
Worse it is, the more they love it.
Want me to prove it?

POET: I don't see any harm in giving miserable people something to
hope for. Just because their clothes zip up the front instead of
buttoning down the back doesn't mean they're happy. They should put
their faith in me, if it helps them any.
(Singsong)
    I say put your faith in me,
    I am like a living tree.

MENCKEN: You've got the Dutch Elm Blight, if you should ask. All you
poets are sick visionaries.

BISHOP: People should put their faith in God, where it belongs. And in the
church, which is the servant of God.

MENCKEN: Eeny, meeny, miny, mo,
Put it in Roosevelt and let it go.

BISHOP: Come, now, the New Deal is a very charitable philosophy. Of
course, they are running the debt up rather high, but one can't count
pennies in the matter of benefaction.

MENCKEN: Count pennies? Those Isaiahs down there can't count three
marbles and make it come out three.
(Intoning)
Ickes, Wallace, Tugwell, Frank,
Take the money from the bank,
Give it to the meek in spirit
Whether or not they have merit.
Have some peruna, Bishop?

POET: What *would* you have the people believe in, Mr. Mencken?

MENCKEN: Mathematics.
I give my clients
Science.
Two and two are four,
Not more.
All their lives people have added numbers together and got
    wrong numbers, because they had a dream.
Poetry is the sleepy weed
The dumb, the sick, and the dizzy need.

POET: I believe in dream. People should have faith in the songs poets sing.

BISHOP: Sing one!

POET: What'll it be?

MENCKEN: Oh, let's have the traditional springtime Nature hocus pocus, and get in a little something about the divine intuitions of poesy. Lull me, in other words.

POET (*Striking a chord on a squash racquet*):
    Earth is a mother, long in labor,
    Brought to bed in a bank of snow,
    Heavy with life—which every neighbor,
    Seeing earth so round, must know.

    Life is a dream of winter's ending,
    Thaw and sap-rise, seed and row,
    I am the midwife, earth attending,
    Bough and bud and fallow doe.

    How shall you pawn the poet's dreaming,
    Knowing not the poet's mind?
    Blackbird swamp, and the meadow teeming,
    Dwell in me and haunt the wind.

    Love in the murmurous pond and peeper
    Girds the lips of maid and lad;
    Follow the march of the freed river,
    Earth is glad, oh, glad!

Swaddling life, in green persuasion,
Frightens some, who dare not speak;
I, the donor, give transfusion
To the wishful and the weak.

Hidden wells of words deep running
Twist my magic willow rod;
Come, I see the turtle sunning,
One with earth, and one with God!

MENCKEN: Well! What do you think of that, Bishop?

BISHOP (*Rubbing his occiput*): Rather nice, I should say; but it has no Authority behind it.

MENCKEN: You mean it's snake oil but it's not your kind of snake oil.

BISHOP: I mean poets are bad communicants. They haven't got what it takes.

MENCKEN: Neither have horse doctors, but people summon them when horses get sick.

POET: Speaking of horse doctors, I haven't heard you mention your favorite yet today, Mr. Mencken.

MENCKEN: Oh, you mean Heywood Broun. I haven't forgotten him, I'm saving him up, the greasy old evangelist.

BISHOP: I don't think he's greasy, I think he's cute.

MENCKEN: Broun, the people's Serious Thinker,
Swallowed Roosevelt, hook, line, sinker.
He feels that Hearst is a moral coward
And draws his paycheck from Scripps Howard;
He's a major bust, a minor prophet,
He's Pepsodent, he's Little Miss Moffet;
He shoots the works for the Newspaper Guild,
He's got the itch and a dumpy build.
What did you start me off on Broun for? Come on out, you
        fellers, and I'll split a bottle of atoms with you. Thank
        God for science at a time like this!
                (They go out, the Bishop rolling rapidly.)

HARPER TO MIFFLIN TO CHANCE

Among the authors who have recently gone to other publishers are H. G. Wells, who left Doubleday Doran for Macmillan; Charles Morgan, author of "The Fountain," who went to Macmillan from Knopf; Harold Bell Wright, who left Appleton's for Harper's; Aldous Huxley, who left Doubleday Doran for Harper's; Louis Bromfield, who left Stokes for Harper's; Tiffany Thayer, who left Claude Kendall for Liveright; and J. P. McEvoy, who went from Simon & Schuster to Houghton Mifflin.

—The Times

Come Harper, come Schuster, come Appleton all,
The winter is coming, and gone is the fall,
The authors are restless and pining to go
And Santa is poorly and we shall have snow!
  Come *on,* Harper!

Come Huxley, come Morgan, come Harold Bell
 Wright,
The dew's on the turnip—the publisher's blight;
Come Bromfield and Thayer, come all God's chillun,
Goodbye to Knopf, sir, and ho for Macmillan!
  Come *on,* Macmillan.

Ho ho! for the writers who pass in the night,
Hey hey! for Al Huxley and Harold Bell Wright,
For the moon on the crest of the newfallen snow
And the luster of Doubleday all in a row.
  Come *on,* Doubleday!

Come author, come poet, come scriveners bold,
The royalty's gone and the days grow cold,
So put on the imprint of Simon & Schuster
And sell a lot more than you formerly uster!
  Come *on,* Simon!

Come Appleton, Harper, come Mifflin and all!
To the top of the list, to the top of the wall!
Your authors are dressed in their last year's loyalty,
They'll kiss you goodbye for the first pretty royalty.
  Come *on,* Pater.

THE LAW OF THE JUNGLE

Mr. Hemingway said that he shot only lions that were utter
strangers to him.

—*The Herald Tribune*

When hot for sport and ripe to kill,
The average novelist shoots at will;
But that, my friends, I'm glad to say,
Is not the case with Hemingway,
Whose sporting life is ever so subtle
Where leopards roam and lions scuttle,
Whose fowling piece doth never bungle
The oldest law of Afric's jungle,
Who stands his ground in time of danger
But only shoots a total stranger.

What sort of cad, I ask, is he
Who meets a cat one day at tea
And next day, in the play of ire,
Cannot control his rifle fire?
Whose morals are so frightfully weird
He dens a lion in his beard
And shoots, to show that he knows how to,
A jungle beast he used to bow to,
Or massacres, in thoughtless wrath,
The first old pal to cross his path?

THE TIMID NAUTILUS

A book, "Under the North Pole," about the Wilkins expedition
will be published shortly by Brewer, Warren & Putnam, Inc.
The book is a novelty, as it is the first time an explorer's story
has been published in advance of the exploration concerned.
                                        —Publishers' announcement

PHILADELPHIA, March 16.—The submarine Nautilus, in which
Sir Hubert Wilkins plans to make a journey to the North Pole,
was beaten back today by a snowstorm in attempting to get
from Camden, N.J., to Marcus Hook, Pa.
                                        —*The Herald Tribune*

Oh, bleak the sky o'er Camden's bourne,
        And dark the cheerless wave and gray,
What time Sir Hubert blew his horn
        And steered for Marcus Hook, Pee A.

The tugs dropped back, the lines came in,
        The wheelsman felt the chilly air,
The Nautilus's screws began
        To churn the threshy Delaware:

The Nautilus of great renown,
        Equipped with every known device,
With rams for knocking icebergs down,
        And knives for boring up through ice,

The Nautilus that must not fail,
        Whose book awaited publication,
The only book to go on sale
        Before the actual exploration.

The tugs dropped back, the lines came in,
        Oh, where away, oh, where away?
Sir Hubert Wilkins soon will gain
        The shores of Marcus Hook, Pee A.

"Is everything aboard?" he cried,
        "All charts, all beef, all mackintoshes?

"Has each of you been well supplied
     "With pens, erasers, and galoshes?"

Awash, awash the winchy rail,
     And bleak the icy windswept river
That held in store the Jersey gale
     That was to make Sir Hubert shiver.

Sir Hubert Wilkins rubbed his hands
     And donned his ulsterette and bowler,
His mind was fixed on colder lands,
     His attitude was bleak and polar.

His work was done, his book was written,
     His publishers had set the day,
And now, in reefer, cape, and mitten,
     He steered for Marcus Hook, Pee A.

His work was done, he paced his boat,
     A smile was on Sir Hubert's face,
The only book that e'er was wrote
     Before the incidents took place.

Abaft the yardage, swathed in blue,
     Sir Hubert paced, all strong and tireless,
And having nothing else to do,
     He sent his publishers a wireless.

"We're leaving," so the message ran,
     "The thirty-ninth degree of latitude."
(His publishers replied at once
     Expressing cheer, good will, and gratitude.)

"Before tonight, despite this squall,
     "We'll bring her safe to Marcus Hook.
"My best to Brewer, George, and all,
     "Regards to Warren. How's the book?"

And thus the conversation went
     In snappy greeting back and forth
Until a snowstorm's quick descent
     Brought ugly tidings from the north.

The wind came sniping through the gear,
  The snow came snozzling down the way,
The helmsman he could hardly steer,
  And where was Marcus Hook, Pee A?

Sir Hubert lashed the boring knife,
  And spiked the rams with heavy marlin,
He quieted the purser's wife,
  And made the sled dogs stop their snarlin.

"The snow is getting worse and worse!"
  He radioed to G. P. Putnam.
The answer came: "Put on your furs
  "And get the second mate to button 'em."

The wind came sniping through the gear,
  The snow came snozzling down the way,
The helmsman through the storm did peer
  But saw no Marcus Hook, Pee A.

Awash, awash the deepy bound,
  And bleak the blizzard they were jammed in,
"We'll turn the Nautilus around
  "And damn well take her back to Camden."

And round they turned her like a top,
  The night was drear and it was snowing;
The expedition had to stop,
  But luckily the book kept going:

The only book that e'er was wrote
  Before its hero sailed away;
The only book about a boat
  Three miles from Marcus Hook, Pee A.

GHOSTWRITING

A course in ghostwriting opens this month at American University, Washington, D.C., and youngsters whose dream is to put words into somebody else's mouth may further their ambition by enrolling. Theirs is a queer dream, but these are queer times. Some university was bound, sooner or later, to make an honest woman out of a ghostwriter, and it's probably no worse than spring football, at that. Dr. Walter P. Bowman, who will teach the course at American, points out that ghostwriters are indispensable today—"indispensable artisans," he calls them. If the course is to face up to realities, Dr. Bowman presumably will not make the mistake of preparing his lectures himself but will locate a behind-the-scenes man on the faculty to get up his stuff for him. The students, for their part, will not waste their own valuable time studying for their exams but will get some bright freshman to come up with the answers.

I've been wondering what sort of final examination would be suitable for a course in ghostwriting. Cyrano de Bergerac, an early ghost, is probably the model to go by. If I were running the shop, I'd require every student, as a condition for passing the course, to compose a ballade while fighting a duel.

"Most of the great speeches we hear," said Dr. Bowman, "are written in whole or in part by someone backstage. It is time we recognized the fact." Well, everyone recognizes the fact that public men receive help in writing speeches, but whether the speeches are "great" is something else again. Roosevelt was a great man and an accomplished actor, but his speeches rarely seemed great to me; they seemed exactly what they were —smooth, carefully contrived, and bravely spoken, right up to the studied reference to God in the final sentence. Because of the nature of radio and television, virtually all public utterances nowadays are prefabricated, and while this tends to raise the general level of expression and gets rid of windbags, it also diminishes the chance of greatness. Great speeches are as much a part of a man as his eyeballs or his intestines. If Lincoln had had help on his Gettysburg speech, the thing would almost certainly have started "Eighty-seven years ago . . ."—showing that the ghost was right on the job.

I did a couple of short hitches, years ago, in the ghost world. A fellow who was trying to interest a syndicate in buying a column patterned after O. O. McIntyre turned the job of writing the sample column over to me. He said he was too busy to do it himself. (Imagine being too busy to imitate O. O. McIntyre!) I had plenty of leisure, and I wrote the column, and the other fellow signed it. I felt ghostly but not unhappy, and in no time at all the syndicate itself became too busy to write checks, and the enterprise blew up, as it well deserved to do. Another time, working for an adman who had motor accounts, I was told that the president of one of the motorcar companies was too busy to write a Christmas piece for the house organ, so I wrote it and he signed it. Here, too, nature took its course. The innocent forgery, so out of key with the spirit of Bethlehem, was presumably discovered by the American public—which is extremely sensitive to such things—and people stopped buying that make of car, and it is now out of existence, as it deserves to be, despite my effort to save it with a poem containing the lines:

> Together we sally at top of the morn,
> With frost on the fender and toots on the horn.

American University, if it is bent on adding ghost training to its curriculum, may soon have to decide how far into the shadowy jungles to proceed. An advertisement appeared in the Washington *Post* recently, reading as follows:

> Too Busy to Paint? Call on The Ghost Artists. We Paint It—You Sign It. Why Not Give an Exhibition?

It turned out that the man behind this enterprise was Hugh Troy, veteran of many a satirical mission. But let no one be fooled. Mr. Troy's jokes go to the heart of the matter; the sober carry on in earnest what he indicates in fun. Essentially, the thing I find discouraging about the ghost world is not its areas of candid dishonesty but that the whole place smells of the American cult of busyness. Too busy to write. Lincoln probably had as much on his mind as the president of the motorcar company, but when an occasion arose, he got out a pencil and went to work alone. His technique is as good today, despite electronics, as it was then. Few men, however, have that kind of nerve today, or that kind of loneliness. They're all too busy taking their ghost to lunch and filling him in.

CALCULATING MACHINE

A publisher in Chicago has sent me a pocket calculating machine by which I may test my writing to see whether it is intelligible. The calculator was developed by General Motors, who, not satisfied with giving the world a Cadillac, now dream of bringing perfect understanding to men. The machine (it is simply a celluloid card with a dial) is called the Reading-Ease Calculator and shows four grades of "reading ease"—Very Easy, Easy, Hard, and Very Hard. You count your words and syllables, set the dial, and an indicator lets you know whether anybody is going to understand what you have written. An instruction book came with it, and after mastering the simple rules I lost no time in running a test on the instruction book itself, to see how *that* writer was doing. The poor fellow! His leading essay, the one on the front cover, tested Very Hard.

My next step was to study the first phrase on the face of the calculator: "How to test Reading-Ease of written matter." There is, of course, no such thing as reading ease of written matter. There is the ease with which matter can be read, but that is a condition of the reader, not of the matter. Thus the inventors and distributors of this calculator get off to a poor start, with a Very Hard instruction book and a slovenly phrase. Already they have one foot caught in the brier patch of English usage.

Not only did the author of the instruction book score badly on the front cover, but inside the book he used the word "personalize" in an essay on how to improve one's writing. A man who likes the word "personalize" is entitled to his choice, but I wonder whether he should be in the business of giving advice to writers. "Whenever possible," he wrote, "personalize your writing by directing it to the reader." As for me, I would as lief simonize my grandmother as personalize my writing.

In the same envelope with the calculator, I received another training aid for writers—a booklet called "How to Write Better," by Rudolf Flesch. This, too, I studied, and it quickly demonstrated the broncolike ability of the English language to throw whoever leaps cocksurely into the saddle. The language not only can toss a rider but knows a thousand tricks for tossing him, each more gay than the last. Dr. Flesch stayed in the saddle only a moment or two. Under the heading "Think Before You Write," he wrote, "The main thing to consider is your *purpose* in writing. Why are you sitting down to write?" And Echo answered: Because, sir, it is more comfortable than standing up.

Communication by the written word is a subtler (and more beautiful) thing than Dr. Flesch and General Motors imagine. They contend that the "average reader" is capable of reading only what tests Easy, and that the writer should write at or below this level. This is a **presumptuous** and degrading idea. There is no average reader, and to reach down toward this mythical character is to deny that each of us is on the way up, is ascending. ("Ascending," by the way, is a word Dr. Flesch advises writers to stay away from. Too unusual.)

It is my belief that no writer can improve his work until he discards the dulcet notion that the reader is feebleminded, for writing is an act of faith, not a trick of grammar. Ascent is at the heart of the matter. A country whose writers are following a calculating machine downstairs is not ascending—if you will pardon the expression—and a writer who questions the capacity of the person at the other end of the line is not a writer at all, merely a schemer. The movies long ago decided that a wider communication could be achieved by a deliberate descent to a lower level, and they walked proudly down until they reached the cellar. Now they are groping for the light switch, hoping to find the way out.

I have studied Dr. Flesch's instructions diligently, but I return for guidance in these matters to an earlier American, who wrote with more patience, more confidence. "I fear chiefly," he wrote, "lest my expression may not be *extra-vagant* enough, may not wander far enough beyond the narrow limits of my daily experience, so as to be adequate to the truth of which I have been convinced. . . . Why level downward to our dullest perception always, and praise that as common sense? The commonest sense is the sense of men asleep, which they express by snoring."

Run that through your calculator! It may come out Hard, it may come out Easy. But it will come out whole, and it will last forever.

BOOK REVIEW
(*Malabar Farm* by Louis Bromfield)

Malabar Farm is the farm for me,
It's got what it takes, to a large degree:
Beauty, alfalfa, constant movement,
And a terrible rash of soil improvement.
Far from orthodox in its tillage,
Populous as many a village,
Stuff being planted and stuff being written,
Fields growing lush that were once unfitten,
Bromfield land, whether low or high land,
Has more going on than Coney Island.

When Bromfield went to Pleasant Valley,
The soil was as hard as a bowling alley;
He sprinkled lime and he seeded clover,
And when it came up he turned it over.
From far and wide folks came to view
The things that a writing man will do.
The more he fertilized the fields
The more impressive were his yields,
And every time a field grew fitter
Bromfield would add another critter,
The critter would add manure, despite 'im,
And so it went—ad infinitum.
It proves that a novelist on his toes
Can make a valley bloom like a rose.

Malabar Farm is the farm for me,
A place of unbridled activity.
A farm is always in some kind of tizzy,
But Bromfield's place is *really* busy:
Strangers arriving by every train,
Bromfield terracing against the rain,
Catamounts crying, mowers mowing,
Guest rooms full to overflowing,
Boxers in every room of the house,
Cows being milked to Brahms and Strauss,
Kids arriving by van or pung,
Bromfield up to his eyes in dung,
Sailors, trumpeters, mystics, actors,

All of them wanting to drive the tractors,
All of them eager to husk the corn,
Some of them sipping their drinks till morn;
Bulls in the bull pen, bulls on the loose,
Everyone bottling vegetable juice,
Play producers jousting with bards,
Boxers fighting with St. Bernards,
Boxers fooling with auto brakes,
Runaway cars at the bottom of lakes,
Bromfield diving to save the Boxers,
Moving vans full of bobby-soxers,
People coming and people going,
Everything fertile, everything growing,
Fish in the ponds other fish seducing,
Thrashing around and reproducing,
Whole place teeming with men and pets,
Field mice nesting in radio sets,
Cats in the manger, rats in the nooks,
Publishers scanning the sky for books,
Harvested royalties, harvested grain,
Bromfield scanning the sky for rain,
Bromfield's system proving reliable,
Soil getting rich and deep and friable,
Bromfield phoning, Bromfield haying,
Bromfield watching mulch decaying,
Womenfolks busy shelling peas,
Guinea fowl up in catalpa trees.
Oh, Bromfield's valley is plenty pleasant—
Quail and rabbit, Boxers, pheasant.
Almost every Malabar day
Sees birth and growth, sees death, decay;
Summer ending, leaves a-falling,
Lecture dates, long distance calling.

Malabar Farm is the farm for me,
It's the proving ground of vivacity.
A soil that's worn out, poor, or lazy
Drives L. Bromfield almost crazy;
Whether it's raining or whether it's pouring,
Bromfield's busy with soil restoring;
From the Hog Lot Field to the Lower Bottom
The things a soil should have, he's got 'em;
Foe of timothy, friend of clover,
Bromfield gives it a going over,

Adds some cobalt, adds some boron.
Not enough? He puts some more on.
Never anything too much trouble,
Almost everything paying double:
Nice fat calves being sold to the sharper,
Nice fat checks coming in from Harper.
Most men cut and cure their hay,
Bromfield cuts it and leaves it lay;
Whenever he gets impatient for rain
He turns his steers into standing grain;
Whenever he gets in the least depressed
He sees that another field gets dressed;
He never dusts and he never sprays,
His soil holds water for days and days,
And now when a garden piece is hoed
You'll find neither bug nor nematode,
You'll find how the good earth holds the rain.
Up at the house you'll find Joan Fontaine.

Malabar Farm is the farm for me,
It's the greenest place in the whole countree,
It builds its soil with stuff organic,
It's the nearest thing to a planned panic.
Bromfield mows by any old light,
The sun in the morning and the moon at night;
Most tireless of all our writing men,
He sometimes mows until half past ten;
With a solid program of good trash mulch
He stops the gully and he stops the gulch.
I think the world might well have a look
At Louis Bromfield's latest book;
A man doesn't have to be omniscient
To see that he's right—our soil's deficient.
We've robbed and plundered this lovely earth
Of elements of immeasurable worth,
And darned few men have applied their talents
Harder than Louis to restore the balance;
And though his husbandry's far from quiet,
Bromfield had the guts to try it.
A book like his is a very great boon,
And what he's done, I'd like to be doon.

A CONNECTICUT LAD

(With a Bag of Popcorn for A. E. Housman)

When first my way to fair I took,
    Danbury's hills were high,
And long I used to stand and look
    At trotting mares go by.

The elms were tall beside the turn
    And sulky wheels were red,
And few the pence that I'd to burn
    And light the heels that sped.

Now times are altered: hills are low,
    And when I take to fair
'Tis likelier lads than I who go
    To stand and watch a mare.

For now that I have pence in bank
    I pause with earnest face
Beside a concrete septic tank
    To drain a country place.

LINES LONG AFTER SANTAYANA

Animal love is a marvelous force.—The Life of Reason

Animal love is a marvelous force,
    According to George Santayana;
It's found in the otter, the coot, and the horse,
And springs from a quite unimpeachable source
    A little this side of Nirvana.
There's hardly a mouse or a ringtailed dove
That hasn't experienced animal love.

Animal love is a marvelous force,
    To which I direct your attention;
It causes the poisonous Gila monster
To govern himself pretty much as he wanster,
    With little regard for convention.
It even induces the people of Wheeling
To heed the imperious call of their feeling.

Animal love is a marvelous force,
    Predestined in life to prevail;
It causes a spaniel from some little distance
To follow the paths of least resistance,
    It quickens the step of the snail.
To cony and starfish and anthropoid ape
It offers the readiest means of escape.

Animal love is the marvelous force
Marsupials take as a matter of course;
You find it in Aryan, Mongol, Norse,
In beetle, tarantula, ostrich, horse;
It creeps in the grasses and blows in the gorse,
It's something all sponges were bound to endorse—
And only in humans it causes remorse.

A LISTENER'S GUIDE TO THE BIRDS

(After a Binge with Roger Tory Peterson in His Famous Guidebook)

Wouldst know the lark?
Then hark!
Each natural bird
Must be seen *and* heard.
The lark's "Tee-ee" is a tinkling entreaty,
But it's not always "Tee-ee"—
Sometimes it's "Tee-titi."
    So watch yourself.

Birds have their love-and-mating song,
Their warning cry, their hating song;
Some have a night song, some a day song,
A lilt, a tilt, a come-what-may song;
Birds have their careless bough and teeter song
And, of course, their Roger Tory Peter song.

The studious ovenbird (pale pinkish legs)
Calls, "Teacher, teacher, teacher!"
The chestnut-sided warbler begs
To see Miss Beecher.
    "I wish to see Miss Beecher."
(Sometimes interpreted as "Please please please ta meetcha.")

The redwing (frequents swamps and marshes)
Gurgles, "Konk-la-reeee,"
Eliciting from the wood duck
The exclamation "Jeeee!"
    (But that's the *male* wood duck, remember.
    If it's his wife you seek,
    Wait till you hear a distressed "Whoo-eek!")

Nothing is simpler than telling a barn owl from a veery:
One says, "Kschh!" in a voice that is eerie,
The other says, "Vee-ur," in a manner that is breezy.
    (I told you it was easy.)
On the other hand, distinguishing between the veery
And the olive-backed thrush

Is another matter. It couldn't be worse.
The thrush's song is similar to the veery's,
Only it's in reverse.

Let us suppose you hear a bird say, "Fitz-bew,"
The things you can be sure of are two:
First, the bird is an alder flycatcher *(Empidonax traillii traillii);*
Second, you are standing in Ohio—or, as some people call it,
    O-hee-o—
Because, although it may come as a surprise to you,
The alder flycatcher, in New York or New England, does not say,
    "Fitz-bew,"
It says, "Wee-bé-o."

"Chu-chu-chu" is the note of the harrier,
Copied, of course, from our common carrier.
The osprey, thanks to a lucky fluke,
Avoids "Chu-chu" and cries, "Chewk, chewk!"
    So there's no difficulty there.

The chickadee likes to pronounce his name;
It's extremely helpful and adds to his fame.
But in spring you can get the heebie-jeebies
Untangling chickadees from phoebes.
The chickadee, when he's all afire,
Whistles, "Fee-bee," to express desire.
He should be arrested and thrown in jail
For impersonating another male.
    (There's a way you can tell which bird is which,
    But just the same, it's a nasty switch.)
Our gay deceiver may fancy-free be
But he never does fool a female phoebe.

Oh, sweet the random sounds of birds!
The old-squaw, practicing his thirds;
The distant bittern, driving stakes,
The lonely loon on haunted lakes;
The white-throat's pure and tenuous thread—
They go to my heart, they go to my head.
How hard it is to find the words
With which to sing the praise of birds!
Yet birds, when *they* get singing praises,
Don't lack for words—they know some daisies:
    "Fitz-bew,"

"Konk-la-reeee,"
"Hip-three-cheers,"
"Onk-a-lik, ow-owdle-ow,"
"Cheedle cheedle chew,"
And dozens of other inspired phrases.

      —E. B. WHITE (gray cheeks,
                inconspicuous eye-ring;
                frequents bars and glades)

THE RETORT TRANSCENDENTAL

In May of the year 1927 I bought a World's Classics edition of *Walden* for, I think, ninety cents and slipped it in my pocket for convenient reading. Since then I have carried it about with me on the cars and in buses and boats, as it is the most amusing detective story I possess. There is, how-ever, a danger in rereading a book, or rather in dipping frequently into the same book: the trouble is you begin to learn some of the lines. In my case, with *Walden,* I have recently found that when someone asks me a simple question I reply with a direct quote.

I go into a restaurant, we'll say, at the lunch hour, and the headwaiter approaches me, accusingly.

"All alone?" he asks.

"I feel it wholesome to be alone the greater part of the time," I reply. "To be in company, even with the best, is soon wearisome and dissipat-ing. I love to be alone." Then I glare triumphantly at the waiter and snatch the napkin from the plate.

Or I am walking along the street and meet an acquaintance—some-one I haven't seen in a long time and don't care if I never see again.

"Where y'been all this time?" he demands.

"If a man does not keep pace with his companions," I retort, "perhaps it is because he hears a different drummer."

Actually, I suppose, I don't say that at all; yet it often seems to me as though I were saying it. More and more I find it difficult to distinguish clearly between what I am saying and what I might easily be saying. Maybe it's the times. At any rate, Thoreau answers a surprisingly large number of the commonest questions that get thrown at me these days. He is a Johnny-on-the-spot for all ordinary occasions and situations.

I enter a room.

"Won't you sit down?" asks my hostess, indicating a vacancy.

"I would rather sit on a pumpkin and have it all to myself," I reply, accepting the velvet cushion with weary resignation.

"What would you like to drink?" she continues.

"Let me have a draught of undiluted morning air," I snarl. "If men will not drink of this at the fountainhead of the day, why, then, we must even bottle up some and sell it in the shops, for the benefit of those who have lost their subscription ticket to morning time in the world." Then I slump into my cushion and wait for the clear amber liquor and the residual olive.

"Know any good books?" my partner asks at dinner. Slowly I swing my head around, bruising my chin on the hard, rough wing of my collar, my eyes glazed with the strain of evening. I place my lips to her ear.

"Much is published," I whisper, cryptically, "but little printed. We are in danger of forgetting the language which all things and events speak without metaphor, which alone is copious and standard."

Or I am at home, getting ready, perhaps, to escort my wife to a soirée.

"What's it like out tonight?" she asks, glancing anxiously at her rubbers in the corner of the closet.

"This is a delicious evening," I hear my voice saying, "when the whole body is one sense, and imbibes delight through every pore."

Next morning, seeing my suit lying rumpled and mussed on the chair beside the bed, she will inquire, "You got anything to go to the presser's?"

"No, my dear," I reply. "Every day our garments become more assimilated to ourselves, receiving the impress of the wearer's character. If you have any enterprise before you, try it in your old clothes." (I am glad to say my wife doesn't mind Thoreau any more and simply calls the presser.)

The situations are endless, the answers inexhaustible. I recall that one of my angriest and boldest retorts was made on a day when a couple of silly, giggling girls arrived at our house and began effervescing.

"Isn't this an attractive place?" they squealed.

"On the contrary," I snapped, "I sometimes dream of a larger and more populous house, standing in a golden age, of enduring materials, and without gingerbread work, which shall consist of only one room, a vast, rude, substantial primitive hall, without ceiling or plastering, with bare rafters and purlins supporting a sort of lower heaven over one's head—useful to keep off rain and snow; where the king and queen posts stand out to receive your homage, when you have done reverence to the prostrate Saturn of an older dynasty on stepping over the sill; a cavernous house, wherein you must reach up a torch upon a pole to see the roof . . . a house whose inside is as open and manifest as a bird's nest."

The girls sobered up instantly and were quiet and tractable the rest of their visit. But I don't know—I'm afraid I shall have to put *Walden* away and buy another book to travel with. Or possibly a link puzzle. One doesn't remember anything much from long association with a link puzzle.

III

ON THE FIELDS

OF

OUR ROOM

FOR SERENA, KEEPER
OF THE DRAW CURTAINS

Evening

At the end of the gift of light, returning,
Draw, with white arm raised, the effective curtain,
Swiftly serry the folds in ranks of twilight,
Strike the camp of the day. Within are burning
Small reliable suns of yellow lamplight
On the fields of our room, where all is certain.

Morning

Slow, the whispering says that night is ended;
Life, awaiting the step of who shall live it,
Threads the chamber of gray and finds the sleeper
Half in doubt of the gift of light intended.
Fling the curtain, Serena, you the keeper
Give the room to the sun, let in the rivet!

LADY BEFORE BREAKFAST

On the white page of this unwritten day
Serena, waking, sees the imperfect script:
The misspelled word of circumstance, the play
Of error, and places where the pen slipped.
And having thus turned loose her fears to follow
The hapless scrawl of the long day along,
Lets fall an early tear on the warm pillow,
Weeping that no song is the perfect song.

By eight o'clock she has rewritten noon
For faults in style, in taste, in fact, in spelling;
Suspicious of the sleazy phrase so soon,
She's edited the tale before its telling.
Luckily Life's her darling: she'll forgive it.
See how she throws the covers off and starts to live it!

RONDEL FOR A SEPTEMBER DAY

Of the white cloud's summer fleece,
    Of the sudden partridge drumming,
Of the cowbell's errant peace
    In a world of cricket strumming—

You, whom I despair of summing
    Up, compounded are of these:
    Of the white cloud's summer fleece,
Of the sudden partridge drumming.

Though the golden meadow cease
    And the grasshopper his thrumming,
You, Serena, still release
    Tidings of another coming
Of the white cloud's summer fleece,
    Of the sudden partridge drumming.

NATURAL HISTORY

(A Letter to Katharine, from the King Edward Hotel, Toronto)

The spider, dropping down from twig,
Unwinds a thread of her devising:
A thin, premeditated rig
To use in rising.

And all the journey down through space,
In cool descent, and loyal-hearted,
She builds a ladder to the place
From which she started.

Thus I, gone forth, as spiders do,
In spider's web a truth discerning,
Attach one silken strand to you
For my returning.

A FATHER DOES HIS BEST

Said I to Lord & Taylor:
    "Hot are the summer skies,
    And my son Joe would like to go
    In a big straw hat in the year-old size.
    Have you got such a thing, for summer skies,
    A nice straw hat in the year-old size?"
Said Lord & Taylor: "No."

Said I to Saks Fifth Avenue:
    "The sunshine hurts Joe's eyes;
    He used to nap in a small white cap,
    But a big straw hat in the year-old size
    Would keep the sunshine out of his eyes.
    Have you got such a thing in the year-old size?"
Said Saks Fifth Avenue: "No."

Said I to Best & Company:
    "I think it might be wise
    When noons are red to cover Joe's head
    With a big straw hat in the year-old size.
    Can you sell me one, if you think it's wise,
    A big straw hat in the year-old size?"
Said Best & Company: "No."

Said I to the infant's mother:
    "It comes as a great surprise
    That our son Joe may never go
    In a big straw hat in the year-old size.
    We had no trouble with his other supplies,
    His Pyrex bottles, his spoon for eating,
    His year-old pot and his year-old sheeting,
    His feeding bib of heavy material
    To catch the spray from the flying cereal,
    Rompers to match the color of his eyes
    In the year-old size;
    These things were bought with the greatest ease,
    The stores were willing and able to please,
    His bands and his year-old shirts all fit,
    His crew-neck sweater and his Arnold-Knit;

I bought him a bear and a rubber cat,
Yet now, when he needs a big straw hat,
I don't know where to go.
Doesn't it come as a great surprise
That there's no straw hat in the year-old size
To keep the sun from the little lad's eyes?"
Said the infant's mother: "No."

THE CORNFIELD

Up to the cornfield, old and curly,
I took Joe, who rises early.
Joe my yearling, on my shoulder,
Observed the old corn growing older.
And I could feel the simple awe
He felt at seeing what he saw:
Yellow light and cool day
And cornstalks stretching far away.
My son, too young and wise to speak,
Clung with one hand to my cheek,
While in his head were slowly born
Important mysteries of the corn.
And being present at the birth
Of my child's wonderment at earth,
I felt my own life stir again
By the still graveyard of the grain.

MEMOIRS OF A MASTER

There were always servants in my father's house, and now there are servants in mine. This morning, from a vantage point in the upstairs hall of my house in the city, I counted five. We have a cook, a chambermaid-and-waitress, a nurse, a laundress, and a furnace man. There are times when amity and peace brood over the home, when the servants remain with us and I begin to have a bowing acquaintance with some of them. There are other periods when the arrivals and departures are frequent and dramatic, and the house takes on the momentous character of the North Beach Airport.

Whenever a new servant is due to arrive, my wife and I always prepare the room for her with our own hands—with a sort of loving suspicion, as you might make a nest for a litter of lion cubs. I have just this minute come from the top floor, where we are fixing up a room for an incoming cook. Her name is said to be Gloria. It sounds implausible; but to me, an old master, nothing is impossible, not even a cook named Gloria. Nothing is even remotely unlikely. I await Gloria with head held high. The encounter with Gloria's bedroom suite, however, has exhausted me; and as I sit here on my study couch, I feel a great wave of fatigue engulf me—the peculiar weariness that afflicts a man who has always had everything done for him. I call it *Meisterschmerz*. I realize that I am not getting any younger and that the day may come when I shall no longer have the physical stamina to be waited on hand and foot by a corps of well-trained domestics.

When bachelors enjoy a reverie, I understand that all the girls of their past float before their eyes in rings of smoke from their pipe. My benedictine smoke dreams are full, not of past loves but of former servants. I dream of Alma, Estelle, Mrs. Farrell, Sylvia, Susan, Anna (who chose a brief interlude with us to have gallstones), Gaston and Eugénie, Elaine the beautiful, Zelda, Otto and Mildred, Mrs. Farnsworth, Joan, Claire. I like to sit here now and dream about them, count them over, like beads in a rosary, and think of all the bright, fierce times I have had with them, sharing their sorrows and their joys, their sickness and their health, taking their phone calls, filling in for them on their days out, driving them to distant churches in remote country districts. They have had some magnificent sicknesses, these old friends of mine, vivid bits of malaise, and truly distinguished indispositions. Every name calls up some bright recollection of bygone days.

Sylvia, for example. Sylvia to me means Christmas, and Christmas in turn means pneumonia. Someone in my family is always sick at

Christmas, and when it isn't I, it is quite apt to be a servant. The year we had Sylvia, it was she. Sylvia had been looking a bit stringy for several days before the twenty-fifth, and we could feel something coming on. We nursed her along and refused to let her do any work, but her fever began on the twenty-fourth, with the early-afternoon carol singing, and rose steadily with the dusk. At last her conversation faded out and she just mumbled something and went to bed. I wasn't feeling any too fit myself, so at six o'clock my wife took first Sylvia's temperature and then mine. Sylvia had me by four and two-tenths degrees, and it was decided that *she* would be the one to go to the hospital. Our doctor verified this and mentioned pneumonia. I simply picked up the phone and said those magic words which I had read so many times on the cover of the directory: "I want an ambulance."

To my astonishment, an ambulance soon appeared in the street below. Police arrived with it, and the living room soon smelled pleasantly of balsam wreaths and Irishmen. The children, of course, adored having police on Christmas Eve—it gave a gala touch to the holiday—but the whole business presented special problems to us parents because all the gifts were hidden in Sylvia's room, and we had the devil's own time keeping the youngsters from running in and out with the cops.

None of us could think of Sylvia's last name, not even Sylvia; but I gave "Cassidy" to the ambulance doctor, and he bundled her downstairs to the waiting car, and away she went through the merry streets, myself following along afoot (with my low-grade fever) like one of the Magi, to attend to the admittance problem—which is part of the servant problem. I shall never forget the hospital's reception of Sylvia. To begin with, the place was jammed—the holiday rush—and the pneumonia ward was full to bursting. Sylvia was rolled into a downstairs corridor and parked there for about half an hour, while sisters of mercy flitted about conjuring up an extra bed. Finally it was arranged, and I accompanied Sylvia up to the ward to tuck her in and wish her a last Merry Christmas, although the poor girl was barely conscious by this time of what was going on. It was after nine o'clock, and the corridor was lit only by a small red night light. Just as our little procession groped its way into the ward, with its dim forms of sickness and the smell of calamity, we were welcomed by a woman's delirious scream.

"Sylvia!" the voice cried, in unworldly pain. "Seeelvyah!" And then a short, rapid "Sylvia, Sylvia, Sylvia," ending with a mournful wolf note, "Seeeeeeelvyah!"

It was the cry of a female who must have had a Sylvia in her family, or in her past, or both. But it was too much for my Sylvia. I think she imagined herself crossed over into purgatory. "Dear God!" I heard her mumble. "Dear God, get me out of here!" Feeling definitely pneumonic myself, and damn sorry for Sylvia and for the world in general, I trudged shakily home and spent the rest of the holy night putting together a child's fire truck, which had arrived from a department store that must have known of our domestic quandary, for they sent the thing in knockdown form—a mass of wheels, axles, bolts, screws, nuts, bars, and cotter pins.

Well, that was all a long while ago. Sylvia pulled through all right, but took a place in the country, where the air would be better for her. I thought, in those days, that I knew what sickness was; but I tell you now that nobody knows what sickness is till he's had an upstairs maid with gallstones. Anna had been with us only six days when her seizure came. In fact, I had never actually seen Anna—her paths and mine never crossed—and I knew her only by hearsay and by the sound of her typewriter tap-tapping on the floor above me. She was an elderly sort, my wife said, with eyes set too near together, like Franklin D. Roosevelt's. I inquired about the presence of the typewriter and my wife explained that Anna had taken up typing, hoping to improve herself. I couldn't very well object, because I had been up to the same trick myself for some years.

Anna, it turned out, was more than a typist—she was a Christian Scientist as well, and she waited grimly through three hours of torture before letting out the yell that began our acquaintanceship. The yell came at four o'clock in the morning, and my wife and I sprang out of bed and instinctively rushed up one flight to see what was the matter.

"Mister," groaned Anna, recognizing me instantly as a friend, "please get me some morphine—it's my gallbladder!"

"Call the doctor!" said my wife. "And," she added peremptorily, "you better get dressed, you may have to go somewhere and you might as well be ready."

As I pattered downstairs, I remember trying to decide between my blue unfinished worsted (whose pockets contained everything necessary for a gallstone operation, such as money, fountain pen, and keys) and my brown tweed, which seemed a more workaday proposition but needed servicing. I knew the day would come and go before I slept again, and I figured I might as well be dressed correctly.

When the doctor arrived, I was fully attired in the blue and ready for anything. He seemed suspicious of Anna's familiarity with morphine, but admitted that her gallbladder might be on the blink and said we'd better get in touch with her relatives. Now, the relatives of domestics are an even more mysterious band of people than domestics themselves. I knew from experience that sometimes they didn't even have names. I also knew that they never had telephones, although they sometimes lived in the same building with a telephone. However, we grilled Anna on the subject of relatives, after the doctor had relieved her, and eventually, by an elaborate bit of telephoning through third parties, we dug up a beauty

—a niece, Anna said she was. We asked her to come as soon as possible. She turned out to be one of the most beautiful women I have ever seen in my life. She arrived about nine that morning, with a fourteen-month-old child in rather bad repair. I let her in, and she immediately handed the baby to me. "Would you mind?" she said. "I have a terrible hangover and can hardly stand up. Isn't it a shame about Bumpo?"

"About who?" I asked.

"Bumpo," she said. "That's what we call my Aunt Anna."

"Oh, I didn't know," I replied. "Yes, it's a dreadful thing, with much pain. I'm sorry *you* don't feel good, either," I added courteously.

"I'll be all right as soon as I get a drink," she said. "I was on a bender last night after the show. I have a walk-on part in the 'Scandals,' you know. Have you seen it?"

"No, but I will," I replied.

Together we marched upstairs. The baby was heavy and soggy, a rather spiritless child. With him in my lap, I made a quick phone call to the office and told them that it didn't look as though I'd be in till afternoon.

I sometimes think that that morning, as I stood around pacifying the grand-nephew of a stricken domestic named Bumpo, my career as a master reached a minor pinnacle, achieved something like nobility. It didn't last, though. Anna had been gone hardly an hour when my wife and I found ourselves engaged in the cheap, vulgar trick of reading the diary which she left behind her. We discovered it on her bureau. Our intentions were honorable enough at first—we were simply thumbing through it hoping to come across her niece's address, which in the confusion she had neglected to leave us. Gradually, however, we became absorbed; Anna's story began to grip us and sweep us along. Written in ink, in a fine, close hand, the diary covered a period of about two years and chronicled her goings and comings in two previous places. For the most part it was a rather dreary recital of a cheerless life. "The madam out this afternoon." "Getting colder." "Robert Taylor was at the Strand yesterday but didn't get to go." We waded, fascinated, through page after page of this commonplace stuff, and suddenly, as though we had been hit across the eyes with a board, we came upon the following terse item: "Phoned Milwaukee police today."

That was all there was to it. Nothing led up to it. Nothing led away from it. It stood there all alone, a tiny purple chapter in a gray little book. We still don't know what it was all about, and we still dream about it sometimes.

Anna had her stones out in good shape and soon grew fit again. We volunteered to pay for the operation, but she refused financial help. Although we held the situation open for her, she never came back to us—which rather disappointed me, as I wanted to get to know her well enough to call her Bumpo. She is probably even now tapping away at her portable machine somewhere—a one-act play, perhaps, or a friendly note to the Department of Justice.

The presence in my house of a group of persons with whom I have merely a contractual relationship is a constant source of wonder to me. Left to my own devices, I believe I would never employ a domestic but would do my own work, which would take me about twenty minutes a day. However, all matters pertaining to the operation of the home are settled agreeably and competently for me by my wife, who dearly loves complexity and whose instinctive solution of any dilemma like marriage is to get about four or five other people embroiled in it. Although the picturesque and lurid role of householder saps my strength and keeps me impoverished, I must admit it gives life a sort of carnival aspect, almost as though there were an elephant swaying in the dining room. And then, once in a lifetime, some thoroughly indispensable and noble person walks casually into one's home, like Antoinette Ferraro, who proceeds to become a member of the family, blood or no blood. Antoinette has been fooling around our house for thirteen or fourteen years, and we would as lief part with her as with our own children. There is no danger of any separation, however. I am perfectly sure that when I draw my last breath, Antoinette will still be somewhere about the premises, performing some grotesquely irrelevant act, like ironing a dog's blanket.

Her name is really Antonietta, and I suspect that I had better not go on with these memoirs without taking her up in some detail, as she is the core of our domestic apple. Without her we should perish; and *with* her (such is the pressure of her outside obligations) we very nearly do. The other night, as my wife and I were sitting by Antoinette's side in the crowded auditorium of a trade school, watching her legitimate son Pietro graduate with honors in my blue serge suit, I had a chance to study the beatific face of this remarkable woman and brood about my good fortune in having encountered her in this world. She was born, I believe, in northern Italy, and speaks an impartial blend of Italian, French, and English. The only form of an English verb which appeals to her, how-ever, is the present participle. In fact, she speaks almost entirely in par-ticiples, joining them by French conjunctions, to which she is loyal. If you ask if she'd be good enough to boil you an egg, her reply is simply, *"Oui,* I'm boiling." Once, on New Year's, she got a little tight on some mulled wine of her own concoction, and when we inquired of her next day if she had reached the Sixth Avenue "El" safely the night before, she blinked her long lashes shyly and said, "Oh, *oui.* Hah! I'm so running! Oh, my!"

Although she ostensibly works full time for us, and gets paid for it, this is merely a mutual conceit on our parts, for she has a full, absorbing life of her own—an apartment full of birds and plants, a son on whom she pours the steady stream of her affection, two boarders for whom she prepares two meals a day, and a thoroughbred Cairn bitch, which (like Antoinette herself) is forever being taken advantage of by an inferior male. The last time this animal had puppies, Antoinette brought one over, tenderly, for us to see. It was something of a monster, with chow characteristics and a set of inflamed bowels. When we offered our condolences on the continuance of the bitch's bitter destiny, Antoinette sighed. *"Ah, oui,"* she said, dreamily. "Wazz that night on the roof."

I marvel that we go on paying Antoinette anything. It takes her two hours and a half to dust one side of a wooden candlestick, and even then she forgets to put it back on the mantelpiece and our Boston terrier carries it to the cellar and worries it in the coalbin. All we gain from the arrangement is Antoinette's rich account of the little adventure, including a perfect imitation of the dog. "He so hoppy," she will explain, "holding in mouth, like beeg cigar, *mais* never dropping. Oh, he barking, he jomping. . . ."

It doesn't sound reasonable, I know, that we should pay anyone to sit around our house and imitate a dog, but we do, nevertheless. One morning she showed up, ready for work, accompanied by a sick bird in a gilded cage, her bitch (again pregnant), and her own family wash, which she always seems to do on our time. "Antoinette," said my wife, exasperated, "I honestly don't see how you expect to do anything for *us* today." Antoinette fluttered her wonderful lashes. "Is all right," she announced, "I'm doing." She never leaves any opening for you at the end of a sentence.

She is a magnificent cook, easily the best we ever encountered, but, because our hours interfere with the proper functioning of her own domestic establishment, she has given up cooking for us and prepares food now only for our dog, kneading raw meat and carrots with kindly red hands and adding a few drops of "colliver oily" as cautiously and precisely as a gourmet fussing over a salad dressing. There have been times when I have looked into the dog's dish with unfeigned envy, for the instant Antoinette's hand touches food, it becomes mysteriously delectable. When I think of her risotto, the tears come to my eyes.

I suppose our affection for Antoinette is temperamental: she likes the same things we do, has the same standards, reacts the same in any situation. She drinks moderately and likes to see other people drink and have a good time; consequently, when you ask her to bring you some ice, she does it with gusto and a twinkle in the eye. We usually manage to sneak her a glass of wine at night, when the other, more straitlaced members of the staff aren't looking. She smokes our brand of cigarettes, and is a chain smoker. She is fond of dogs, and indeed is the only domestic of my acquaintance whose first concern, when a dog is sick on the rug, is for the dog. I can't help liking that in her, even though I often have to clean the rug myself while she is comforting the animal. If you give her an old flannel shirt to launder, she lavishes all her love and skill upon it, and it comes back to you the same size as when it went to the tub. And then, Antoinette has that great Latin quality: she is a realist. Life is life, and it's the way it is. We had a manservant one time—a middle-aged Belgian who went hog wild one morning about ten o'clock, kicked pots and pans all over the pantry, and wound up by taking off all his clothes and running naked up and down the laundry, hoping by this sudden noisy revel to engage Antoinette's fancy. Neither my wife nor I was home, and when we apologized later to Antoinette for this unexpected bit of goatishness, she chuckled reminiscently. "La, that old fellow," she snickered. "Is nothing."

This same old fellow who was nothing was my first experience with a manservant. His name was Gaston, and his career with us was brief but colorful. He was one half of a "couple," and nobody has had any experience of a domestic nature till he has employed a couple. I was against the idea, but my wife assured me that a couple would be more economical because then the man could tend the furnace. Unimpressed by this flimsy bit of logic, I went to a nursemaid then in our employ and asked her if she had ever worked in the same house with a couple. "Oh, sure, I like it," she replied. "It's fun to come down in the morning and see which one has the bruises."

I really held out for quite a while against a couple.

"But why?" asked my wife doggedly. "What earthly reason is against it?"

"Well," I said, "I'm not going to have any man pussyfooting around this house, bowing and scraping."

"What's wrong with a man?"

"Well, I don't know," I cried, "it's just sort of immoral, that's all."

"Immoral! What kind of crazy reason is that? It's no more immoral than having *you* around."

"You know what manservants do sometimes, don't you?" I asked.

"What do they do?"

"They steam open your letters. I saw one do it in the movies one time."

"Oh, my God," said my wife, and the talk ended. Gaston and Eugénie arrived the following Monday, in a cab.

They were, as I have said, Belgians. It seemed to me then, and still seems, an inspired bit of deviltry on my wife's part to engage a couple neither of whom could speak or understand English. I myself neither speak nor understand any other language. I can usually grasp Antoinette's meanings, because she puts in a liberal dash of English participles and nouns. Gaston and Eugénie spoke a mixture of French and

Flemish, which gave even my bilingual wife a little trouble. In fact, until Gaston and I worked out a system of arm signals and small guttural cries, there was practically no communication between any of us in the home.

"He'll soon learn English," my wife assured me. And indeed the old fellow did make a stab at it. One evening, after a formal dinner party at which Gaston had officiated, we men stepped out into the garden for a smoke while the ladies withdrew, genteelly, to the living room upstairs. I was half through a cigarette when Gaston appeared in the garden, his bald streak shining in the moon, his gray curls festooned like tiny vines around his big, rascally ears. With his index finger pointing upward, he placed his heels neatly together, bowed, and said, *"Pardon, M'sieu. Café* oops."

"How's that, Gaston?" I said sheepishly, while my fascinated guests watched. *"Café* what?"

"Café oops, *M'sieu.* Oopstair."

"Ah, oui. Ah, oui, Gaston," I replied glibly, and led the gentlemen aloft to their coffee.

In the long roster of persons who have been attached at one period or another to our house, Gaston and Eugénie were far from being the most successful, but they were in many ways the most distinguished. The head of the employment agency where my wife found them had been most enthusiastic—they were the "perfect servants" and had been trained in the household of a Washington diplomat, an ambassador, I believe. I think my wife was just a shade impressed by this. Anyway, she failed to foresee the unhealthy effect it would have on Gaston to go straight from serving an ambassador to serving a screwball like me. I was always rather sorry for the old boy, with his courtly manner and his bucktoothed little wife, who grinned and said yes even when she didn't understand what you said, which was always. The very first meeting between Gaston and myself was unpropitious and drab. I had a rotten cold on the Monday when he arrived, and spent the morning wrapped in an old button-up-the-front sweater in my third-floor study among some diseased house plants and empty picture frames. My wife left early in the morning, to be gone all day, and had given instructions to the breathless new couple to prepare for me, the unseen master, a lunch, explaining that I was unwell, in the chambers above, but would descend to the dining room for the noon meal.

"M'sieu est grippy," she said, in her best Flemish.

"Oui, Madame," Gaston had replied respectfully.

At one o'clock, I heard stealthy footsteps outside the door, then a rap. "Yes?" I said. The door opened, and there he was—a faded, gray little man, beautifully if unsuitably attired in tails. There was something tragic about the appearance, in my dismal doorway on a Monday noon, of a Belgian husband in evening dress. Against the peeling plaster walls, he looked wrong, and I knew then and there that our adventure with a couple was ill-starred. His skin was a cigarette-ash gray, and his bow tie was not much less dingy. Having been instructed by my wife never to address me in French or Flemish, and being incapable of announcing lunch in any other tongue, he simply raised one arm in a long, eloquent sweep toward the stairs and the smell of meat balls, and departed.

Lunch turned out to be a considerably gayer occasion than I reckoned on. I was joined at table by my small son, Bertrand, and our Boston terrier, Palsy. The latter, far from being depressed by the sight of a tailcoat at noontide, was exhilarated. He took up a wing-back position near the woodbox and executed a brilliant series of line bucks through Gaston's skinny legs. Ordinarily, Bertrand would have welcomed a free-for-all of this sort with howls of encouragement, but to my amazement the little boy sat spellbound and quiet, his steady gaze never wavering from Gaston's contorted features, his grave demeanor in strange contrast to Palsy's clowning. There was something genuinely compelling in Gaston's hauteur, and throughout the meal Bertie spoke only in whispers. I kept blowing my nose and scolding Palsy, but there wasn't much use in it. Finally I said to Gaston, "I am sorry, Gaston, that the little dog attacks you foolishly. Soon he will get to know you."

"M'sieu?" queried Gaston, trembling with incomprehension.

"The little dog," I said, pointing. "I fear he is a great trouble to you."

Gaston considered this speech carefully, searching for meanings. Then his features composed into a hideous smile. Picking up a meat ball between thumb and forefinger, he bent stiffly from the waist and handed it to Palsy, dreaming, I do not doubt, of his life in Washington, among decent people.

When we fired Gaston and Eugénie for Gaston's vile interlude in the laundry, he put on quite a scene, at first refusing flatly to accept the dismissal. I stood by while my wife alternately discharged him in French and translated his protests to me in English. We were, he said (and his great, melodious voice dipped deep into the lower register and then swooped up again like some dark bird), making the supreme mistake of our lives, dispensing with the services of himself and his so talented wife. We countered. Liquor, we said, had unquestionably debased him. Eugénie, hearing the word "liquor," nodded violently in agreement: liquor had made Gaston gross, but we should not concern ourselves with such harmless derelictions. Gaston grew more and more surly. A discharge was out of the question, and he was willing to lay the whole unfortunate affair to our inexperience as master and mistress of a household. "He says we're inexperienced, darling," said my wife.

This, for some reason, made me mad, for I remembered Anna's gall-stones and a thousand and one other nights. "By God, nobody's going to stand there and call me inexperienced!" I shouted. "You get out of here, you lecherous old scarecrow."

Half an hour later they were gone, but not before Gaston had got in the last word. He appeared on the second-floor landing with his trunk, set it down, and turned to salute us.

"S'il faut partir, il faut partir. Pfui!" And with a quick little push, he launched the trunk into the air and watched it go roaring down to the floor below, chipping off pieces of stair as it went. Thus departed the perfect servant.

My wife is not easily discouraged, and Gaston and Eugénie were followed closely by another wedded pair, Otto and Mildred. They were young Germans, but they spoke English clearly enough—it just came natural to them. Otto was the *Turnverein* type, big, blue-eyed, vain, and strong; well-being oozed from every pore. I always felt that he should wear shorts and a small rucksack when waiting on table. He loved moving heavy objects, because it showed off his strength, and he frequently went down cellar and threw boxes and crates around for no particular reason. When my Aunt Helen, who is a fairly fleshy old lady, returned to our house to convalesce after she'd had her appendix out, the problem came of getting her upstairs. "Dot's nudding," said Otto, appraising her quickly. And before any of us could stop him, he gathered Aunt Helen in his arms, scar tissue and all, and bounded up two flights of stairs with her. "So!" he said, plopping her down on the bed.

Otto loved to be in the same room with me. When he discovered I was a writing man, he determined to be of the greatest possible assistance to me, and was always busting into my study, clad in a zipper campus jacket and bearing a greasy clipping from the *Daily Mirror.* "Here's a tchoke for you," he would announce, handing me some unattractive oddity in the news, such as a cat mothering a baby robin. I had to give up trying to work at home during the time he was with us. I used to go to the reading room of the Public Library and sit with other escapists at long oak desks.

There is something about our household which invariably makes it seem like a comedown to servants after other houses they have been in. Gaston and Eugénie were gravely disappointed that our home wasn't an embassy. Otto was crushed when he found out I didn't own two Duesenbergs. The man he worked for just before he came to us had two Duesenbergs, and Otto kept throwing them in my face. Even had I allowed Otto to drive my old Hudson sedan, which I never did, I'm sure it wouldn't have filled the void in his life. I think it was the humdrum of our home that drove him into aviation as a sideline. He managed to combine the two vocations charmingly—waiting on table here and spending his Thursday and Sunday afternoons off at an airfield in Flushing, taking flying lessons.

I asked him if it wasn't pretty expensive. "Na," he replied. "Ten dollars an hour, dot's all." His goggles, which he showed me one day, cost $27.50.

He progressed rapidly in the air. When he got so he could solo, he used to fly across the river and circle above our house, banking sharply at the prescribed altitude and showing off as much as he could without violating the Bureau of Air Commerce regulations. It was a perfect outlet for his Aryan spirits, but it was just one more straw for my tired old back. I got damned sick of hearing the drone of my employee's plane over my rooftop, and I never got quite used to having my Friday-morning coffee poured by a man lately down from the skies. I felt earthbound, insignificant, and stuffy; and I began to compensate for this, unconsciously, in my attitude toward Otto.

"Well," I would say sourly, "I see you didn't break your neck yesterday."

Otto would laugh—a loud, bold laugh. "Na, I'm too schmart."

He *was* too smart, too. He left our household not as the result of any aerial mishap but because he couldn't get on with Bertrand's nurse, Katie, a pretty little Irish girl who called him Tarzan behind his back and was no more impressed by his gorgeous torso than I was.

I guess Otto's most notable quality was his readiness to answer all questions, at table. We first noticed this in him the day Aunt Helen went to the hospital for her appendectomy, which was very soon after Otto's arrival.

"I wish I knew how much the operation is going to cost," I remarked to my wife at dinner.

"Fifty dollars," replied Otto, coming up on my left with a dish of broccoli.

I was delighted at this sign of alertness in him and soon discovered that his store of information covered every subject. If a guest, for example, filled in a dull pause at dinner by remarking that she had found a terribly nice little flower shop but she couldn't remember whether it was on Fifty-first Street or Fifty-second Street, Otto would pipe up, "Fifty-first." If you speculated as to what theater a certain show was playing in, Otto would announce, "Broadhurst."

I never knew him to be right about anything, but he was an enormous comfort just the same. There are lots of times when you like to get a quick answer, even though it means nothing.

Another thing I rather enjoyed about Otto was his identification with the world of crime. Otto hadn't been with us three days when a jeweler's wife was murdered in a small suburban apartment building by a lover in a state of pique.

"It's funny how dot feller got in her hallway," said Otto, taking a quick glance over my shoulder at the newspaper.

"What's so funny about it?" I replied. "He got in by pushing somebody else's bell and walking in when they clicked."

"Dot's what *you* think," said Otto. "But dot building ain't dot way. You godda be let in."

"How do you know so much about it?"

"I worked there."

It soon became clear that Otto had worked not only at the scene of that crime but at the scene of all crimes. While police wallowed in the darkness of an unsolved mystery, Otto and I walked in the light of exact knowledge. I consulted him whenever I was in doubt about any point, and always got a direct, clear answer.

Smoke dreams! How charmingly these dear people drift before me as I sit here with my pipe and my memories! I think back to the soft spring evening, ten years ago, when I was in the dining room lingering over coffee. The door opened and a young peasant woman entered, carrying a dustpan full of horse manure. It was some which she had discovered in front of the house, following the fitful passage through our street of a Borden's delivery wagon. The young woman, surprised to find me still in the dining room, blushed prettily, then carried her treasure out into the back garden and spread it tenderly on the exhausted little plot of soil which supported our privet bush.

The smoke curls in wreaths around my head. I see the thin, competent form of Mrs. Farrell, whom Antoinette always called Farola and who in turn called me Dearie. I think of Minnie, the Bahai, whose piety allowed her to partake of food only before sunrise and after sundown, and whose abstinence so weakened her that she used to run the eggbeater in the kitchen to drown out the noise of her lamentation. And of Mrs. Farnsworth, the aged eccentric, whom, in the course of a five-hundred-mile motor journey, I regaled with a dollar-and-a-quarter chicken dinner only to see her sweep the entire contents of her plate off into her purse, to take to the little dog that was the delight of her life.

I count them over, one by one. Today, however, I feel a great lethargy creep over me. Sometimes I wish I could relive all those strange and golden times; but there are other moments, when the radio is particularly loud in Francine's room and the *Meisterschmerz* is strong upon me, when I know that all I want is peace.

CALL ME ISHMAEL*

Or, How I Feel About Being Married to a Bryn Mawr Graduate

This is a ridiculous assignment. The sensations of a Bryn Mawr husband are by their very nature private. Even if there were some good excuse for parading them in public, a prudent male would hesitate to make the attempt, so greatly do they differ from common sensations. But as far as that goes, a prudent male wouldn't have married a Bryn Mawr girl in the first place—rumors would have reached him of the wild fertility revels that take place on May Day, of the queer ritual of the lantern, of the disorderly rolling of hoops, and of all the other racy symbols and capers of the annual Elizabethan hoedown. A sober male, sifting these disturbing tales of springtime debauchery, quite properly would have taken stock of the situation. A girl who has spent her senior year dancing around a Maypole and beating a hoop might easily take a lifetime to cool off. A prudent male would have boarded the first train for Poughkeepsie and sought out some simple, modest maiden with daisies in her hair.

I do not, in fact, recommend that any young man enter into a marriage with a Bryn Mawr girl unless he is sure he can absorb the extra amount of emotional experience that is involved. To awake to a serene morning in a green world; to be overtaken by summer thunder while crossing a lake; to rise bodily from earth, borne aloft by the seat of one's pants as a plane passenger is lifted from the runway—unless a man can imbibe these varied and sometimes exhausting sensations, can profit from them, can survive them, I recommend that he take the easy course and marry into Wellesley or Barnard or Smith. But if he is ready for anything, if he wants to walk straight into the jaws of Beauty, if he aspires to rise above the fruited plain and swing by his heels from the trapezes of the sky, then his course is clear and the outskirts of Philadelphia are his hunting ground.

Bryn Mawr graduates, in their appearance and their manner and their composition, are unlike all other females whose minds have been refined by contact with the classics. They have long hair that flows down over their bodies to below their waist. They rise early, to sit in the light from the east window, brushing their tresses with long, delicious strokes and then twisting them into an intricate series of coils and loops and binding them with pins made from the shells of tortoises or, more lately, from the plastics of Du Pont. The husband's day thus begins with the promise of serenity, of order. But there is nothing static about Bryn

*Editor's Note: Early in 1956, the editor of the Bryn Mawr *Alumnae Bulletin* invited White to set down his impressions of being married to a Bryn Mawr graduate. White complied with the request, the piece was published in the Summer 1956 issue of the *Bulletin*.

Mawr. As the day advances, the pins grow (as though nourished by the soil of intellect), thrusting up through the warm, lovely hair like spears of crocuses through the coils of springtime. When fully ripe, the pins leap outward and upward, then fall to earth. Thus does a Bryn Mawr girl carry in her person the germinal strength of a fertile world. Once a week she makes a trip to a hairdressing establishment that used to go by the name of the Frances Fox Institute for the Scientific Care of the Hair, where she is restored and cleansed by three ageless nymphs named Miss Abbott, Miss Nelson, and Miss Robinson, usually (as near as I can make out) while sitting in a booth next to the one occupied by Lillian Gish.

Bone hairpins are not the only things that fall, or pop, from a Bryn Mawr graduate. There is a steady cascade of sensible, warm, and sometimes witty remarks, plus a miscellany of inanimate objects, small and large, bright and dull, trivial and valuable, slipping quietly from purse and lap, from hair and ears, slipping and sliding noiselessly to a lower level, where they take refuge under sofas and beds, behind draperies and pillows—pins, clips, bills, jewels, handkerchiefs, earrings, Guaranty Trust Company checks representing the toil of weeks, glasses representing the last hope of vision. A Bryn Mawr girl is like a very beautiful waterfall whose flow is the result of some natural elevation of the mind and heart. She is *above* paper clips, above Kleenex, above jewels, above money. She spends a large part of each day *making* money and then comes home and rises above it, allowing it to fall gently through the cracks and chinks of an imperfect world. Yogi Berra would be the perfect husband for a Bryn Mawr girl, but I am no slouch myself; I have come a long way in the catcher's art and am still improving my game.

I have known many graduates of Bryn Mawr. They are all of the same mold. They have all accepted the same bright challenge: something is lost that has not been found, something's at stake that has not been won, something is started that has not been finished, something is dimly felt that has not been fully realized. They carry the distinguishing mark —the mark that separates them from other educated and superior women: the incredible vigor, the subtlety of mind, the warmth of spirit, the aspiration, the fidelity to past and to present—girls like Helen Crosby, Diana Forbes Lloyd, Laura Delano Houghteling, Evelyn Shaw McCutcheon, Claire Robinson, Nancy Angell Stableford, Emily Kimbrough, Elizabeth Shepley Sergeant, Sheila Atkinson, Evelyn Washburn Emery, Edwina Warren Wise, Frances Fincke Hand, Cornelia Otis Skinner. What is there about these women that makes them so dangerous, so tempting? Why, it is Bryn Mawr. As they grow in years, they grow in light. As their minds and hearts expand, their deeds become more formidable, their connections more significant, their husbands more startled and delighted. I gazed on Pembroke West only once in my life, but I knew instinctively that I was looking at a pile that was to touch me far more deeply than the Taj Mahal or the George Washington Bridge.

To live with a woman whose loyalty to a particular brand of cigarettes is as fierce as to a particular person or a particular scene is a sobering experience. My Bryn Mawr graduate would as soon smoke a cigarette that is not a Parliament as sign a check with an invented name. Not long ago, when a toothpaste manufacturer made the wild mistake of changing the chemical formula of his dentifrice, he soon learned the stuff Bryn Mawr is made of. My wife raised such hell that our pharmacist, in sheer self-defense, ransacked the country and dredged up what appears to be a lifetime supply of the obsolete, but proper, paste.

You ask me how I feel to have undertaken this union. I feel fine. But I have not recovered from my initial surprise, nor have I found any explanation for my undeserved good fortune. I once held a live hummingbird in my hand. I once married a Bryn Mawr girl. To a large extent they are twin experiences. Sometimes I feel as though I were a diver who had ventured a little beyond the limits of safe travel under the sea and had entered the strange zone where one is said to enjoy the rapture of the deep. It was William Browne who most simply and accurately described my feelings and I shall let him have the last word:

> Briefly, everything doth lend her
> So much grace, and so approve her,
> That for everything I love her.

PETER HENDERSON IN FLORIDA

(A Letter to Katharine, from Palm Beach)

From this fat garden, with its slow noon beat,
Its steady shadow and its clinging heat;
From careful palm, from white & blinding wall,
From sleepless lizard & the hot vine's scrawl,
From tropic luxury and southern sweetness
My senses turn (seeking their stern completeness)
To you, my love, & to our northern spring—
Crosby's Egyptian, and the Golden King!

Suggested name for largest
tomato in the world—
M. Ridiculosa

WEDDING DAY IN THE ROCKIES

The charm of riding eastward through Wyoming
Is not so much the grandeur and the view
As that it is an exercise in homing
And that my fellow passenger is you.
In fourteen years of this our strange excursion
The scenic points of love have not grown stale
For that my mind in yours has found diversion
And in your heart my heart could never fail.

It's fourteen years today since we began it—
This sonnet crowds a year in every line—
Love were an idle drudge if time outran it
And time were stopped indeed were you not mine.
The rails go on together toward the sky
Even (the saying goes) as you and I.

TO MY AMERICAN GARDENER, WITH LOVE

(For Katharine's birthday, September 17, 1961)

Before the seed there comes the thought of bloom,
　　The seedbed is the restless mind itself.
Not sun, not soil alone can bring to border
This rush of beauty and this sense of order.
Flowers respond to something in the gardener's face—
Some secret in the heart, some special grace.
Yours were the rains that made the roses grow,
And that is why I love your garden so.

EXPECTANCY

The grass at night is sweet in country places,
In honor of green morrows yet to be;
The little stream slides bright through moonstruck spaces,
In fond anticipation of the sea.
Beneath a hill, low in the drowsy willows,
A hundred frogs invisible and clear
Have propped themselves on green convenient pillows
To blow their flutes and say that spring is near.

But not the sweet grass hopeful of the day,
Nor moonbright stream with all its happy humming,
Nor fluting frogs that sit up nights to play
And warn the waiting world of what is coming,
Shall know or feel or sing the expectant song
I sing who wait where you will walk along.

EARLY SONG

Waking to the bird chorus
Arranged for us—
The robin and the bright sparrow
Saying Good Morrow,
And the fretful crow
With his particular woe—
I await, in the dissolving dark,
The whispered first remark,
Reach out (groping
    Sleepily hoping)
The hand toward hand:
Then, hearing no word said,
Finding no fingertip across the bed,
Am slowly, sadly aware
You are not there.

SONNET

That same white traveler, frost, that could not pass
And not leave everywhere his lovely scroll,
Having sufficiently adorned my glass,
Painted your portrait on my secret soul.
Thus you've been with me all this winter day,
And I, who love myself, went two and two,
My actual solitude a seeming play
Built of the meaning and the breath of you.

You in each item of this day of fearing
All thoughts I wanted to—and could not—tell;
You in the log of pine, you in my hearing
The cold and lonely ringing of a bell.
Your voice at sundown, swelling, repeating, thinning,
Lost in the hurrying night and the wind's beginning.

IV

WHAT

YOUTH

MUST

FIGURE

OUT

YOUTH AND AGE

This is what youth must figure out:
    Girls, love, and living.
    The having, the not having,
    The spending and giving,
And the melancholy time of not knowing.

This is what age must learn about:
    The ABC of dying.
    The going, yet not going,
    The loving and leaving,
And the unbearable knowing and knowing.

CONCH

Hold a baby to your ear
    As you would a shell:
Sounds of centuries you hear
    New centuries foretell.

Who can break a baby's code?
    And which is the older—
The listener or his small load?
    The held or the holder?

CHAIRS IN SNOW

Quiet upon the terraces,
    The garden chairs repose;
In fall they wore their sooty dress,
    Now the lees of snows.

How like the furnishings of youth,
    In back yards of the mind:
Residuals of summer's truth
    And seasons left behind.

TREES OF WINTER

Oh, they are lovely trees that wait
 In the still hall of winter,
 Silent and good where the Good Planter
Fixed the root, wove the branch delicate.

Friendly the birches in the thin light
 By the frost sanctified,
 And here, too, silent by their side
I stand in the woods, listening, upright,

Hearing in the cold of the long pause
 Of the full year
 What trees intend that I should hear:
Interpretations of old laws . . .

Hearing the faint, the chickadee cry
 Of root that molders,
 Of branch bent, and leaf that withers,
And little brown seed that does not die.

IT'S SPRING, SPRING
IN PITTSFIELD, MASS.

It's spring, spring in Pittsfield, Mass.,
    Track and slide go bare;
It's raining hard in many a pass,
    And balmy blows the air.

The thaw has come to Pinkham Notch,
    It's forty-nine in Stowe;
Up, crocus, up! Come, slip, come, vetch!
    We'll sprout before we go.

It's slush, slush in Intervale,
    The ski is on the rack,
The snow train threads the greening dale
    With sun upon its back.

It's spring, spring in Montreal,
    Laurentian lads are hot;
Old winter on his knees shall crawl.
    I say, "Why not, why NOT?"

SPRING PLANNING

Let the sun go on if it will, promising much;
Let earth respond, lift up foolishly,
Try the power of her recovered sweetness
And give of her swamp smells.
Let the new sun go on, promising much,
I'll not go along this time.

I think I've had enough of hopefulness,
Green things and promises, new things and promises;
Rather than go through that once more,
Knowing spring comes to no good end,
Rather than rehearse the whole long show again like a child,
Knowing the story well, knowing the ending, my mind running on
   ahead,
I'll try another plan:
I'll wear September like a charm all spring—
The dry grass,
The dead wind,
Love pitched in the wrong key,
The fading color,
The brown last act of the play Ecstasy—
I'll turn my face away in time, my heart averted safe,
Then let earth try me!
Let earth tempt me with a face that is beautiful
(I think I've seen that face before),
With lips that smell sweet, of new things;
Let earth turn loose all her tricks—it will make no difference:
The marauding soldier bee, possessing the white flower in the sun;
The hen, brooding warmly, bulging her warmth to the eggs;
I'll not see nor hear them, pay no attention
To frog celebrants in the night, green tunes from offstage choruses,
No attention to crow calling,
To the valley alive with mystery,
To the surrounding hills alive again with love of the mysterious
valley.

It's not the first time.
Once, I remember, there was a girl
Cruel as earth, bright as the new spring.

What if there was? I knew the sweetness was too short—
Short, clear as a bird-note, trailing away,
Leaving the air empty and still, the heart empty,
Leaving the heart blistering to that year's harvest sun,
Trying foolishly to cry to that year's harvest moon, finding no tears.
Where is the love, I said, that's worth love's ending?
Where the brightness worth the resultant gray?
The fierce glad season worth the death of it?

I say I have a better plan:
Let the sun go on, promising much,
Posting its love letters on the east wind—
I'll tear them up,
I think I'll tear them up.
I'll tear them up . . . very gently.
I do not think I am afraid to tear them up.

THE TENNIS

Circled by trees, ringed with the faded folding chairs,
The court awaits the finalists on this September day,
A peaceful level patch, a small precise green pool
In a chrysanthemum wood, where the air smells of grapes.
Someone has brought a table for the silver cup.
Someone has swept the tapes. The net is low;
Racket is placed on racket for the stretch.
Dogs are the first arrivals, loving society,
To roll and wrestle on the sidelines through the match.
Children arrive on bicycles. Cars drift and die, murmuring.
Doors crunch. The languorous happy people stroll and wave,
Slowly arrange themselves and greet the players.
Here, in this unpretentious glade, everyone knows everyone.
And now the play. The ball utters its pugging sound:
Pug pug, pug pug—commas in the long sentence
Of the summer's end, slowing the syntax of the dying year.
Love–thirty. Fifteen–thirty. Fault.
The umpire sits his highchair like a solemn babe.
Voices are low—the children have been briefed on etiquette;
They do not call and shout. Even the dogs know where to stop,
And all is mannerly and well behaved, a sweet, still day.
What is the power of this bland American scene
To claim, as it does, the heart? What is this sudden
Access of love for the rich overcast of fall?
Is it the remembered Saturdays of "no school"—
All those old Saturdays of freedom and reprieve?
It strikes as quickly at my heart as when the contemptuous jay
Slashes the silence with his jagged cry.

FALL OVERCAST

There's a horn on the play.
There's a haze in the dell.
Dakin will kick.
Hooper will hold.
The hills are in gray.
The air will turn cold.
Fumble.

There's a haze in the dell.
The ball's on the ten.
He got it away.
There's a horn on the play.
Hoogin will hold.
Caskey will kick.
Are your hands cold?
Your feet?

DeLoosey for Wrenn.
The year's at the close.
The ball's on the ten.
He fades, throws.
The pass is complete.
Goal.
The wind blows
And blows.

The hills are in gray.
Someone will kick.
Someone will hold.
The year has grown old.
They made it.
A minute to play.
A gain of two yards.
The game has grown old.
An overcast day.
A sweet, sad day.
They're leaving the stands.
It's over.

ON BEING ASKED FOR "A STATEMENT"

Statement of what, sweet Prince? What need be stated?
My health? My health is good, but who's the wiser?
Eyes gray, hair brown; such things are overrated.
My work? Work is a jade, yet youth doth prize her.
Or would you have me, homing, greet the press:
Predict the upturn just around the corner,
Foretell the color of the autumn dress?
"My next film is 'The Kiss,' produced by Warner."

Come, come, my Prince, viewed from 'most any angle
Such neat brown thoughts are but the winter birds
That skirt and scatter in the spiky tangle
Which is the mind, for which we have no words.
A statement you must have? 'Tis your own choosing.
Let's see. . . . Well, how is this? *Life is amusing.*

INCIDENT ON A CAMPUS

Returning to the college town
    And sitting in the room,
I saw the neatly folded hills,
I heard the blessing of the bells;
    And looking south and looking west
Watching the light that crowned the hills,
    I waited to be blest.

But steadily up the long street
    In endless file the students came.
I saw the students striding by,
I saw them walking home from classes
    One and one
      And two and two
   . And three and three
Eagerly,
Strong and resolute and sad,
Firm and gay and brave and fair,
And it was more than I could bear
    That none of them was I,
    That not a one was I.

Abandoning the stale room,
    Tasting the bitter cup,
As one in dream I set my feet
To trail the students up the street,
    A ghost recruit.
Silent I walked among the living.

The elms saw. The walls spoke.
The valley signaled me in smoke.
And at the crashing of the hour
The bells, applauding from the tower,
Granted my need for an abatement,
Wildly retracted every statement.

And suddenly
I turned and faced the ones advancing—
A hundred students passed me by
And every one was I,
Oh, every one was I.

THE ANSWER IS "NO"

What answer maketh the crow?
Always "No."

Put several questions in a row
To a crow,
You will get "No, no, no,"
Or "No, no, no, no."

Sometimes, on being questioned,
The crow says "Naw"
Or "Caw."
But regardless of pronunciation,
There is never anything but opposition, denial,
And negation
In a crow.

In their assemblies at the edge of town,
Crows introduce resolutions, then vote them down.
How many times in summer, waked early by the mosquito,
Have I lain listening to the crow's loud veto!

Once, gunning, I wounded a thieving
Crow
And have not forgotten his terrible, disbelieving
"Oh, no!"

ZOO REVISITED

Or, The Life and Death of Olie Hackstaff

I. THE BUFFALO RANGE

Pause here, my soul, and pause then here my son, which art my soul,
Here stands the finished bison by the last water hole.
Here sleeps entombed forever in the brown sensate robe
The seminal imperative in the suspended globe.
Low droops the bearded head and low the small and hateful eye;
The plains where burned the fires of dung are dust and the trails are
    dry.
Here stands incarcerate the bull, with his expended fire,
Bos americanus in the twilight of desire.
Here stands the bull Myself, alone, with his torrential need,
At home with living death, at rest with reservoirs of seed;
Pause here my self, my soul, my son, by this encrusted rail. . . .
    Don't put your mouth on that dirty old rail!

II. END OF MORNING AT BEGINNING OF LIFE, HOME FROM SCHOOL

It's quarter of twelve.
It's fourteen of.
It's thirteen of.
It's twelve of.
The bell will ring in just a sec.
"Dismissed," she'll say. "Dismissed.
Boys, when you go to the cloakroom,
    please
        don't
           shove!"
It's twelve of, it's twelve of,
And still she clings to the short division
(Where the chalk squeaked, the pointer motioned)
    Divider
    Dividend
    And quotient.
    (The product of the divider and the quotient should equal the
dividend.)

There it goes!

The peak of the cap is the visor, unsnap it then snap it,
The peak of the cap . . . unsnap it then snap it.

(Step by step and flag by flag avoiding crack and
block by block the small boy Olie makes his way in
young September's quiet street by hedge and yard
and stoop and drive where blue hydrangeas sadly sway
and grapes are purpling in the arbor:

home is a haven
home for lunch
home is a harbor.)
   (Kenny Whipple says turtles lay eggs.)
By hedge and yard and stoop and drive.
I can't wait.
I have to go.
Do they lay eggs or don't they?
. And if they do, how do they?
   (because where would?
   even if . . .)

Why does an older boy like Kenny
Laugh when he tells the rabbit's story?
Why does he hang around the hutch
Where something happens that you have to know—
Something the buck does with the doe,
Something that's sad and terrible to know?
   (Everybody has to know.)

I can't wait.
I have to go.

By hedge and yard and stoop and drive:

The Belknaps.
The Gants.
The Immelmans.

Do they lay eggs or don't they?
And if they do, how do they?

Five more houses five more hedges five more . . .
They couldn't possibly.

because where would?
even if.

Home is a harbor,
Home for lunch.

III. BY THE SEA

This is my get, proprietor, and this the doe.
Have you a room for us who fear the sea?
I am the small boy redivivus, this is me.
Give us a room with bureau space to grow.

"Take Mr. Hackstaff to three nineteen!"

Knock at the door, my bucko, swing her in!
Observe the bed, the chair, the chair, the bed!
Come smell the bureau drawers!
I tarried here a while when I was thee.

Open the drawers take off your things take off
    your coat put on your sneaks throw up the
    sash unpack your bag hang up your coat!
Run a little water in the basin,
I want you to get your hands clean!

(For what? Were my hands clean in those days?)

Sit down here and put your sneaks on!

(How well I know this sultry scene
where dreaming summer takes her toll
her cruel toll
this sadly overwritten scene
when summer takes complete command
belly to sun and back to sand
how well I know these mourning streets
the lawns the privet and the rose
the bay and the way the wind blows
the tide ebbs and the tide flows
the salted skin the burning air
the combed scalp the sand in hair
oh windblown scene oh dune and mallow . . .)

The spacious ballroom is ideal for dancing

His name was redivivus
And they called him Red for short.
   "I'm checking out of three nineteen.
   Will you send a boy for the bags?"

   IV. THE SWORD

"Make me a sword!"

(Man lives alone and by the sword.)
"What for? [You mean for the wars, the debatable wars?] You get
the stick from the cellar."

"For the scabbard?"

"No, for the sword."

"You have to saw a piece off, to nail across, and smooth a place where
my hand goes around."

"The grip?"

"Smoothened for the hand, the edges rounded."

"This stick is dusty. Get a cloth. Don't dust
   it here it'll dirty the room take it out
   and dust it not with that new cloth it'll
   ruin it."

"Where is the saw?"

"Hold it, hold the end."
   (The first stroke, sawblade against thumbside. On
   this point, my hearty, impale the world. "Hold
   the end while I saw a piece off." On this point,
   which isn't even sharpened yet, impale the enemy
   only don't get hurt. "Hold it steady and don't fool.")

   (Man lives alone and by the sword,
   youth dreams alone and girds for right
   and dulls his blade against the stone;
   the dream fails in the short night.
   Man is disarmed and still alone.)

keep your feet dry
don't take cold
be polite shake hands with Mr. Hecatomb
marry a nice girl
pay your bills
look at those hands
don't put your mouth on that dirty old rail

V. LIEBESTRAUM

It is at night, when the old woods are still,
The weedy pond first feels the winter's chill.
    (Now night be still and let the cold
    Seal fast the wintry pond!)

Still pond, no more moving!

It is in youth there comes, and one time only,
This dream of love, this flowerform of light,
Perfect in deed and wanting no completion
    (Now youth be still and let the dream
    Seal fast the faithful heart!)

Still pond, no more moving!

VI. THE HOSPITAL

When the grass is long is the time for dying.
Did you know that, nurse?
Death is a wind that rustles our estate,
Turning up fourteen pairs of ecru curtains,
Number forty-eight in the catalogue.
(Bend down, librarian, and taste the page!)
Here is the printed list—the end of Ivy Hall.
Contents of Bedroom Number One, leaving behind
    to the hammer's fall
Five pairs summer blankets, three single blankets—
    Oh sandtoy summer in the mind
    The star (of tin)
    The fish (of tin)
    The crescent moon (of the best quality tin)—
Bend down, librarian, and taste the page,
I'm checking out of three nineteen.
Death is a wind that rustles the estate.

And welcome to the zoo, my dear,
The reptile house, the serpents tonguing
With all their hateful coils of longing,
The lidless eyes the darkness holds
In its own long and scaly folds.
Don't put your mouth on that dirty old rail, nurse!
    When the grass is long is the time for dying,
    The grass was a cradle when I was child,
    The grass was the bed I had as lover.
    My first instruction was from the clover
    In the wise field.
    The grass was my portion when I was lean,
    The warmth in the grass is a gift to the lonely;
    The ranks of the leaves were broken only
    For me and trouble to pass between.
    The grass is my need in this last embrace
        (When the grass is long is the time for dying)
    My blood is drink for the roots that are drying,
    The strength of the seed is around my face.

don't run with a knife
keep back from a scythe keep back from a saw
when you lean out of the window keep your
        weight low, on the inside.

Low and on the inside, eh, announcer?
Bend down, librarian,
The page is me, and gently hold the place.
    (Notice: These seats are for the
    exclusive use . . .)
And for the Belknaps, the Gants. Do they lay
        eggs or don't they?
Bos, his name is. In the bullpen.
Bend down.
Keep your weight low, nurse, and on the inside.

        "Dr. Ternidad! Dr. Breese!
        Dr. Ternidad! Dr. Breese!"

THE STREET OF THE DEAD

When they came to Eleventh Street, on their way to school, the little boy said to his father, "Is this the street with the graveyard?"

"Yes," said the man.

"Can we go through it, please, so I can see the graveyard?"

"Let's go through Twelfth Street," said the man, "and I'll show you a house I used to live in years ago."

"I want to see the graveyard with dead people." He pulled at his father's hand, and as was often the case with the man and his four-year-old, the little boy got his way—not by being rude or obstreperous but by a certain superior force of character, a certain intensity. They turned into Eleventh Street. The man realized that he had given in, but he half suspected that in such a matter the child had a right to his own prejudices.

The father rather enjoyed these early morning trips to school. The dog always went along, a sturdy black animal with an idiot love of life. They made an odd trio: the dog tugging hard at the leash; the little boy, hampered by thick leggings, dragging behind; the man a twisted but happy link between them, letting the dog supply the motive power for all three—swept through the chill winter streets at a quarter to nine, the man's hastily swallowed breakfast not sitting any too well, his eyes not yet focusing clearly.

"Is that it?" cried the little boy, breaking into a gallop. "Look, Daddy, there's a grave!" They had arrived at the tiny cemetery near Sixth Avenue, a triangular plot where two or three underfed trees sheltered the sparse dead of the Spanish and Portuguese Synagogue. Dreary above the hard-packed mud rose the headstones; between them lay some fragments of broken glass and old candy wrappers. A cat moved slowly along the brick wall at the rear.

"There's another grave!" cried the child, his cheeks pressed against the iron bars of the gate.

"Look at that big ol' cat up there on the wall," said the man. "That's some cat!"

"Is it dead?" asked the little boy.

"No, it's alive," said the man. Then he added: "Alive and well."

"If I died would they put me in?"

"You're not going to."

"Would they bury me?"

"Yes. We better hurry or we'll be late for school." The child hugged the iron gate tightly; his grip was strong.

"If I fell out of our window would I die?"

The man calculated the vertical distance, saw the toppling child, saw the fall, the crowd, the pavement, the people staring, saw the report of the ambulance surgeon.

"Yes," he replied. "Come along now, son."

They pulled away. The dog whirled them on, out of danger, into life again. They crossed over the street, and up a block, and over to school. The man went in with his son and accompanied him up three or four flights of stairs to the play yard on the roof. He stood for a moment in the doorway, talking to the teacher. She was a short woman, with a kind heart and flashing eyes.

"We're very enthusiastic about Elliott," she said.

"So am I," said the man, absently.

"At first he had a tendency toward over-stimulation, but he's beautifully adjusted now."

"That's good," said the man, who was having a little trouble with the dog.

"Elliott really makes such good use of his information," she continued.

"His information?" echoed the man, dreamily. He watched his son pick up a wooden block and heave it.

"We try to direct all their little energies toward inventive things, so that they have an immediate creative object. You see, children have a tendency to try to solve social situations."

"They do?"

"Yes, and that's bad."

"Of course."

"We have one little girl here, and at first she was interested only in tackling adult problems and social situations. She doesn't happen to be here today with the group—she strained her knee playing, and the doctor said she might as well stay home, because it hinders her in Rhythms."

"That's too bad," said the man.

"It's wonderful how she has come around, I mean about not trying to solve social situations. But children are like that. It's just a question of getting at them and knowing what they're all about."

"I suppose it is."

He said goodbye, his eyes lingering on his son for a parting look. Led by the idiot dog, he scrambled downstairs and out into the street. He put on his hat, jerked it down over his eyes, started for home at a fast clip, no little boy dragging this time. Homeward journeys were made in record time, the dog in high. It was just a question of getting back to the apartment, slipping the leash, taking another sip of cold coffee, gathering up the newspaper, and starting uptown to work. At the corner of Eleventh the dog, remembering the cat in the cemetery, pulled hard, trying to force a turn into the block. The man yanked back. "Come on!" he muttered angrily. The dog continued to strain, the collar gagging him.

"Come on, come on, you crazy bastard!"

The man jerked the protesting animal along; and together they went home, through Tenth, each wrapped darkly in his own thoughts.

V

NO PEOPLE

OF NO

IMPORTANCE

DUSK IN FIERCE PAJAMAS

Ravaged by pinkeye, I lay for a week scarce caring whether I lived or died. Only Wamba, my toothless old black nurse, bothered to bring me food and quinine. Then one day my strength began to return, and with it came Wamba to my bedside with a copy of *Harper's Bazaar* and a copy of *Vogue*. "Ah brought you couple magazines," she said proudly, her red gums clashing.

In the days that followed (happy days of renewed vigor and reawakened interest), I studied the magazines and lived, in their pages, the gracious lives of the characters in the ever-moving drama of society and fashion. In them I found surcease from the world's ugliness, from disarray, from all unattractive things. Through them I escaped into a world in which there was no awkwardness of gesture, no unsuitability of line, no people of no importance. It was an enriching experience. I realize now that my own life is by contrast an unlovely thing, with its disease, its banalities, its uncertainties, its toil, its single-breasted suits, and its wine from lesser years. I am aware of a life all around me of graciousness and beauty, in which every moment is a tiny pearl of good taste, and in which every acquaintance has the common decency to possess a good background.

Lying here in these fierce pajamas, I dream of the *Harper's Bazaar* world, the *Vogue* life; dream of being a part of it. I fancy I am in Mrs. Cecil Baker's pine-paneled drawing room. It is dusk. (It is almost always dusk in the fashion magazines.) I have on a Gantner & Mattern knit jersey bathing suit with a flat-striped bow and an all-white buck shoe with a floppy tongue. No, that's wrong. I am in chiffon, for it is the magic hour after bridge. Suddenly a Chippendale mahogany hors-d'œuvre table is brought in. In its original old blue-and-white Spode compartments there sparkle olives, celery, hard-boiled eggs, radishes—evidently put there by somebody in the employ of Mrs. Baker. Or perhaps my fancy wanders away from the drawing room: I am in Mrs. Baker's dining room, mingling unostentatiously with the other guests, my elbows resting lightly on the dark polished oak of the Jacobean table, my fingers twiddling with the early Georgian silver. Or perhaps I am not at Mrs. Baker's oak table in chiffon at all—perhaps instead I am at Mrs. Jay Gould's teakwood table in a hand-knitted Anny Blatt ensemble in diluted tricolors and an off-the-face hat.

It is dusk. I am dining with Rose Hobart at the Waldorf. We have lifted our champagne glasses. "To sentiment!" I say. And the haunting dusk is shattered by the clean glint of jewels by Cartier.

It is dusk. I am seated on a Bruce Buttfield pouf, for it is dusk.

Ah, magazine dreams! How dear to me now are the four evenings in the life of Mrs. Allan Ryan, Junior. I have studied them one by one, and I feel that I know them. They are perfect little crystals of being—static, precious. There is the evening when she stands, motionless, in a magnificent sable cape, her left arm hanging gracefully at her side. She is ready to go out to dinner. What will this, her first of four evenings, bring of romance, or even of food? Then there is the evening when she just sits on the edge of a settee from the Modernage Galleries, the hard bright gleam of gold lamé topping a slim, straight, almost Empire skirt. I see her there (the smoke from a cigarette rising), sitting, sitting, waiting. Or the third evening—the evening with books. Mrs. Ryan is in chiffon; the books are in morocco. Or the fourth evening, standing with her dachshund, herself in profile, the dog in full face.

So I live the lives of other people in my fancy: the life of the daughter of Lord Curzon of Kedleston, who has been visiting the Harold Talbotts on Long Island. All I know of her is that she appeared one night at dinner, her beauty set off by the luster of artificial satin and the watery fire of aquamarine. It is all I know, yet it is enough; for it is her one perfect moment in time and space, and I know about it, and it is mine.

It is dusk. I am with Owen Johnson over his chafing dish. It is dusk. I am with Prince Matchabelli over his vodka. Or I am with the Countess de Forceville over her bridge tables. She and I have just pushed the tables against the wall and taken a big bite of gazpacho. Or I am with the Marquis de Polignac over his Pommery.

How barren my actual life seems, when fancy fails me, here with Wamba over my quinine. Why am I not to be found at dusk, slicing black bread very thin, as William Powell does, to toast it and sprinkle it with salt? Why does not twilight find me (as it finds Mrs. Chester Burden) covering a table with salmon-pink linens on which I place only white objects, even to a white salt shaker? Why don't I learn to simplify my entertaining, like the young pinch-penny in *Vogue,* who has all his friends in before the theater and simply gives them champagne cocktails, caviar, and one hot dish, then takes them to the show? Why do I never give parties after the opera, as Mr. Paul Cravath does, at which I have the prettiest women in New York? Come to think of it, why don't the prettiest women in New York ever come down to my place, other than that pretty little Mrs. Fazaenzi, whom Wamba won't let in? Why haven't I a butler named Fish, who makes a cocktail of three parts gin to one part lime juice, honey, vermouth, and apricot brandy in equal portions—a cocktail so delicious that people like Mrs. Harrison Williams and Mrs. Goodhue Livingston seek him out to get the formula? And if I *did* have a butler named Fish, wouldn't I kid the pants off him?

All over the world it is dusk! It is dusk at Armando's on East Fifty-fifth Street. Armando has taken up his accordion; he is dreaming over the keys. A girl comes in, attracted by the accordion, which she mistakes for Cecil Beaton's camera. She is in stiff green satin, and over it she wears a silver fox cape which she can pull around her shoulders later in the evening if she gets feeling like pulling a cape around her shoulders. It is dusk on the Harold Castles' ranch in Hawaii. I have risen early to shoot a goat, which is the smart thing to do in Hawaii. And now I am walking silently through hedges of gardenias, past the flaming ginger flowers, for I have just shot a goat. I have on nothing but red sandals and a Martex bath towel. It is dusk in the Laurentians. I am in ski togs. I feel warm and safe, knowing that the most dangerous pitfall for skiers is *color,* knowing that although a touch of brilliance against the snow is effective, too much of it is the sure sign of the amateur. It is the magic hour before cocktails. I am in the modern penthouse of Monsieur Charles de Beistegui. The staircase is entirely of cement, spreading at the hemline and trimmed with padded satin tubing caught at the neck with a bar of milk chocolate. It is dusk in Chicago. I am standing beside Mrs. Howard Linn, formerly Consuelo Vanderbilt, formerly Sophie M. Gay, formerly Ellen Glendinning, formerly Saks Fifth Avenue. It is dusk! A pheasant has Julian Street down and is pouring a magnificent old red Burgundy down his neck. Dreams, I'm afraid. It is really dusk in my own apartment. I am down on my knees in front of an airbound radiator, trying to fix it by sticking pins in the vent. Dusk in these fierce pajamas. Kneeling here, I can't help wondering where Nancy Yuille is, in her blue wool pants and reefer and her bright red mittens. For it is dusk. I said *dusk,* Wamba! Bring the quinine!

THE KEY OF LIFE

One of the people affected by England's suspension of the gold standard was Henry C. Earp, who didn't understand what it meant. He simply knew that the news made him feel queer. He read it on his way to work, riding down on the El. The El made Mr. Earp sick in the early morning anyway: this morning the combination of England's crisis and the train's motion gave him the sort of indigestion that is part fear and part jiggling.

There had been so much talk about bad times; Mr. Earp had even heard the words "revolution" and "panic." Those words came back to him. Here was England, suspending the gold standard. That might mean anything. It might mean (Mr. Earp said the word softly to himself) "everything." Through his head there flashed a succession of cataclysmic events—fighting in the streets, mill riots, fire, bank failures, dissolution of all the things that made a civilized people. He trembled as the El train rattled along. What if everything were really coming to an end? Suppose the dollar should drop in value till it was just so much paper—where would he be? Quite possibly the only survivors would be persons who owned their own land and grew their own food and made their own clothes out of the skins of animals. Mr. Earp allowed his mind to rest, for a fleeting moment, on the possibility of his shooting an animal and making a suit of clothes from the skin.

He also ran over in his mind the years that had flown by, the eighteen years that he had been pleased to regard as his business career. His really wasn't a career at all. He had never made any money, had merely held his job. The Little Birdseye Furniture Company hadn't advanced him, nor had they fired him. He ran the tickler cards in their credit department; he knew which installment customers to dun and which to let alone. Eighteen years had taught him the exact moment at which to call up and say that the Company would send its truck to take away the davenport unless a substantial payment were made. But he hadn't actually advanced any; and now, while England tottered, he was still making thirty-two dollars a week. Maybe in a week's time thirty-two dollars wouldn't be worth the paper it was printed on. Mr. Earp was thoroughly frightened.

A few minutes before he arrived at his station, he happened to glance again at his newspaper, and his eye lit on an advertisement that won his close attention. A man was going to lecture that night at Carnegie Hall, on "Making Your Life a Supreme Success." He would divulge business secrets and tell *how to get ahead seven times faster.* It was to be a free lecture, Mr. Earp noticed. Another subhead challenged him: "Excusefinders not wanted; if you think the depression is going to last forever, we can't help you!"

Mr. Earp liked the tone of that. Somebody, at any rate, wasn't scared. The train stopped and he got out and walked to the office, his stomach still bothering him.

That evening, at 8:15, he was at Carnegie Hall. He found a balcony, and sat there, in the half-seat high in the topmost section of the darkness, holding, with some embarrassment, the little folder the usher had handed him, "Making Your Life a Supreme Success." The hall was crowded. This fellow must be pretty good. Mr. Earp looked about, shyly, at the people around him. Some were men his own age, behind whose pale brows rested the neat and tired brain of the desk worker. Some were young couples, obviously searching for life's key. He saw a white-haired man of seventy, blind in one eye. He saw a colored man with a carnation in his buttonhole. All were eagerly staring down toward the far-away stage where the Success Builder, in evening dress, was beginning his talk. Mr. Earp glanced nervously through the little folder. There were pictures of the successful graduates of the Complete Course, now out in life making good: happy branch managers, happy sales executives answering busy telephones, happy captains of field artillery, and one happy old lady who had commercialized her fruit cake at the age of sixty-one. There were letters of congratulation from the governors of states, and there were extracts from newspapers quoting the speaker as an authority on business. At the end there was a coupon to be filled out by those who wished to "go on" to the real twelve-part twenty-dollar course; and a money-back guarantee for the unsatisfied.

Earp was excited. The crowded hall, the sense of being on the verge of something, set his blood going. Again he felt sick, but this time it was the nausea of renascent hope. He was listening to a big man, a man who had made good, a man who wasn't worried about the gold standard. Earp collected his attention.

"The world," he heard the great voice say, "is full of good things, and you can live a full life, every one of you. But my friends, has it ever occurred to you that the people who get the good things in this world are the people who have been *trained* to get them? Why, I was reading only the other day about the star players of the Notre Dame team, coming back for fall practice. You might ask: Why should last year's football stars have to practice for the 1931 season—why don't they sit back and take it easy? My friends, I'll tell you why: It's because this is 1931, not 1930. And next year will be 1932, and I say to you that if you go into 1932 with a 1931 mind, then you will deserve to fail!"

Mr. Earp gripped his seat. This man was talking a man's language, no vague nonsense.

"Now another thing," continued the speaker, "you've all heard a great deal of loose talk about the depression. A man came to me the other day and said he'd been to a crystal gazer, and the crystal gazer had said to him: 'Don't start anything till after the first of April.' My friends, *I* say that anybody who postpones his plans for six months will forget he ever wanted anything."

There was a ripple of applause, in which Mr. Earp, tucking his folder under an arm, joined. When the applause faded, the speaker read a poem called "When I Appreciate You and You Appreciate Me" and then took up, one by one, the twelve "tool" subjects that would be covered in the Coaching Course: How You Can Win Immediate Advancement; How to Acquire Popularity, Poise, and Power; How to Express Yourself to Win; and so on. The speaker's voice was becoming richer, more emotional. He told pertinent story after pertinent story, parable after parable, all pointing the same moral. Earp's eyes glistened. He chuckled at the stories, nodded his head wisely at the parables. This was the greatest lecture he had ever heard.

It was getting late, and the speaker went into his conclusion—a long story about his childhood. When he was a child, farmers always stored apples in their cellars in winter. Some of the apples were good apples, and some were specked apples; and when he, as a little boy, used to go down cellar he was always told to bring up the specked apples for eating, otherwise they would spoil. But of course there was always a new lot of specked apples every time, so the result was that his family went all winter eating the specked apples, never eating the good apples. "My friends," he said, "there are hundreds of men and women in this great auditorium tonight (and I regret that so many other hundreds had to be turned away at the door) who are leading specked-apple lives! Are *you* leading a specked-apple life? I say to you that the world is full of good things, and you who are content to eat specked apples because you don't *know enough* to eat the good ones are losing the richest joys of this great, rich, abundant earth."

The applause was heavy. Mr. Earp rose with the others. His legs felt strong under him. He had forgotten England and her sorrow, forgotten the Little Birdseye Furniture Company. This was a different world—a gorgeous place of lights, people, and intimations of big events. He was at the stairs. As he began the long slow descent to the lobby, his exhilaration was almost unbearable. The people in his path seemed to block him, prevent him from getting started.

At the bottom of the first flight of steps, a young man with curly black hair turned casually to him and said: "The same old boloney, eh?"

Mr. Earp swallowed. He nodded weakly, without looking at the youth.

"Success stuff is always the bunk," continued the young man. "It's all in getting a break. A corporation doesn't recognize an individual."

"Sure, I know it," said Earp, a trifle sullenly.

"What a bunch of horsefeathers that guy spilled—all them jokes about specked apples and all that junk!"

"I'll say," said Earp. His tone was more positive.

They descended another flight, slow step by slow step. The curly-headed youth still stuck to him. "I'm sorry for the saps that fall for a spellbinder like him, and pay good money for the course."

"You and me, brother," said Earp, with a slight vocal swagger.

They reached the lobby and passed quickly by the desks where people were signing up for the twenty-dollar complete course of twelve steps that would enable them to become successful in business. At the sidewalk, the two parted. Earp crossed Fifty-seventh Street and got on a bus. The conductor, noticing that he had come from the lecture, nodded his head toward Carnegie Hall.

"You been in there?"

"Sure," said Earp.

"How was it? Did that feller tell you anything?"

Mr. Earp was halfway up the stairs to the upper deck of the bus. He turned, sagely. "The usual horsefeathers," he replied.

THE SEVEN STEPS TO HEAVEN

On a critical afternoon in July, with the suffering city hanging in the balance outside his window, Dr. Joseph Link stood by the air conditioner in his office, enjoying the two-minute breather he allowed himself between patients. He switched the machine to EXHAUST and lit a cigarette. A wispy vision of lung cancer drifted lazily into his mind as the smoke curled downward into the vent and disappeared. Who would his next patient be, in the long, long procession? A Mrs. Mooney, the card said. Mrs. Edward Mooney. What part of Mrs. Mooney would hurt? Where would her agony lie? What organ was deranged, what function failing? The short recess passed all too quickly. Dr. Link got rid of his cigarette, switched the machine back to COOL, sat down at his desk, and buzzed. Sure enough, a Mrs. Mooney appeared—a fabulously commonplace little woman. Cute as a bug, he thought. Warm as a rose. Healthy, desirable, worried, eager to begin.

"Is it just the profanity?" asked Dr. Link a few minutes later. "Or does your husband have other disturbing habits?"

"His habits aren't really so bad," said Mrs. Mooney. "I mean, in some ways he seems normal enough. But the swearing is getting worse. If we had children, I don't know what . . ."

"How violent is it?"

"I can't tell you the words, Doctor. I couldn't possibly imitate Ed."

"Does he swear *at* something in particular?"

"Oh, yes," replied Mrs. Mooney. "There are a number of things that ruffle him. Is it true, Doctor, that extreme profanity is an indication of mental trouble? I read that in the paper. He gets so worked up over nothing."

"Give me an example."

"Well, do you ever look at the late news on Channel Two?"

The doctor shook his head.

"Do you ever watch the Giants?"

"I'm afraid not. They're behind, aren't they?"

"Of course. But that isn't the point. The Giants are different than most teams, Dr. Link. I mean, you'd really have to see what happens, from time to time. Ed watches television a lot, Doctor. He doesn't like the little man going up the steps."

"Little man?" said the doctor. "What little man?"

"The one carrying the wand. I tell Ed it's nothing to get so sore about. This little fellow marches up a flight of stairs, raising his knees very high, like a drum majorette, while the music goes down the scale. Ed can't stand him. He starts swearing and yelling and—"

"Why does that irritate him?" asked the doctor.

"I don't really know. I sometimes think beer has become a symbol of defeat for Ed—on account of associating them together? The Giants mean a lot to my husband."

"What else irritates him?" asked the doctor.

"The word 'birdbrain.' It's applied to Mr. Bocker when he does something stupid. I don't see why Ed should care so deeply. And he doesn't like the name on the letter box, either."

"What letter box?"

Mrs. Mooney sighed. Everything would be so much easier, she thought, if doctors were conversant with real life.

"It's part of a humorous commercial," she said patiently. "Ed doesn't like funny stuff, Dr. Link. He hates the humorous way the bottle of beer suddenly appears in Mr. Bocker's hand. With that pinging sound? I wish you could hear Ed, Doctor. It literally burns up the inside of your ears. It's frightening. That's why I'm here—I'm so frightened. Ed worries about the deeper meaning of things, and I think it makes him sick. 'Louise,' he said to me, 'what is going to happen to a nation when the people are rewarded for an act of stupidity with a cool refreshing drink?' Just worrying about civilization can make a person sick, can't it?"

"Very sick," replied Dr. Link. "What else doesn't he like?"

"Jean Sullivan for Blue Cross."

"Do you and your husband carry medical insurance?"

"Oh, no," said Mrs. Mooney. "Ed hates the guts of anything like that."

"Why?"

"Well, you know how she starts a sentence with 'You see—' as though she was really talking to you and being cozy?"

"Who?"

"Jean Sullivan. She's the pretty one. Do you know what Ed told me once? He said an expression like 'you see' is all worked out in advance by writers who know just when to put it in—to make it sound casual. Ed says he bets some of those writers are very sick men themselves, sicker than they realize. 'God damn it, Louise,' he said, 'I bet some of those writers have a liver that is as hollow as an old jack-o'-lantern.' Only he was much more profane than that."

"You say she's pretty?"

"Who?"

"This Jean Sullivan."

"Well, she's certainly prettier than Bill Rigney, and Ed can't stand him, either. You know how, when there's a double play, they send two thousand cigarettes to the veterans' hospital?"

"No, I didn't know that."

"Well, they do. The other night in the game with the Phillies, they had Lockman on second with two out, the way it always is, and they needed runs bad. Don Mueller hitting .226 is up, with Mays coming up next, and Rigney takes Mueller out and sends in Jablonski to face Simmons, who is a left-hander. 'That's wrong, Louise,' Ed said to me. 'Rigney should of left Mueller in.' You see, Ed has a different philosophy about baseball than Rigney. I guess you would call Ed very unorthodox. He believes that there are intangible factors which enter into a situation like this, like how does Rigney know Jabbo wasn't out last night eating a bad clam and can't even see as far as the end of his bat. Ed says you have to have an instinct for the imponderables if you are going to manage a ball team. He uses the word 'imponderables' quite a lot. Well, as it turned out, Ed was right and Rigney was wrong. Jablonski went down swinging—a curve ball."

"You were talking about the veterans' hospital, Mrs. Mooney."

"I know. Well, Ed can usually tell what will happen to the Giants before it takes place; he just seems to know what is going to take place, and of course it drains a person emotionally. If you could hear the words he uses about Rigney. I think Ed is very sick. He broods and broods about the veterans. He told me once he was thinking of writing what he called a monograph on the relationship of the double play in major-league baseball to the incident of lung cancer in males. He said it would make a goddam good title."

Dr. Link smiled. "I hope he'll send me a copy."

"Don't worry, he won't ever write it," said Mrs. Mooney. "Ed talks a lot but he almost never does anything he says he's going to do. But I love Ed, Doctor. There are some things I agree with him about, too, only I don't see why you have to get so worked up. Like about Russ Hodges's shirt? I don't care for the shirt, either—the plaid is awfully big. But so what?"

Dr. Link felt the conversation slipping again. He found himself feeling mildly annoyed by this patient—a woman he had never seen before, coming in cold and putting her husband's sanity up to him. His professional duty was clear, however; he must listen to her story, give her a bit of reassurance, and then urge her to send her husband in for examination. The hum of the air conditioner was an irritant. The doctor got up and switched it off.

"Of course," continued Mrs. Mooney, "I've known for a long time there was something queer about Ed—ever since the day he used the carbon paper and it went off on its own."

"Did what?"

"Ed wrote a letter, Doctor. It was a letter applying for a job, and he wanted to keep a copy, so he inserted a piece of carbon paper in the typewriter. Usually he gets it in backwards—I mean upside down—so it just marks up the other side of the original?—but this time he got it in right. I saw the copy with my own eyes. I saw it myself, so I know this is true."

"Saw what, Mrs. Mooney?"

"Well, the first paragraph of his letter came out the same as the original, but the second paragraph was an account of the seventh inning of the game between the Giants and the Cubs."

"Are you saying that your husband wrote one thing on his typewriter and something quite different appeared in the carbon copy?"

"No, just in the second paragraph. The first paragraph was O.K. Antonelli started for the Giants in that game and he was pulled out in the seventh. Ed was a little surprised himself when he saw the carbon, but he didn't say much. He just stared at the carbon copy and said, 'The times are out of joint, Louise.' "

"Did he get the job?" asked Dr. Link, whose attention had been jogged by this part of the narrative.

"No, he didn't. He's had to hang around home, day in, day out. I guess the day the delicatessen made the mistake in my order was the worst. That was what really convinced me I had to see a doctor. It was really fantastic, because this man that runs the delicatessen knows Ed well and I just can't believe he would have done what he did intentionally even if he *was* all out of Prior's dark beer. Ed and I were watching TV—an afternoon game. Ed wasn't working, as I have explained, Doctor. That's another thing he blames Rigney for. Anyway, the Giants were coming to bat in the bottom of the eighth with the Braves leading four to nothing and the doorbell rang and it was the boy from the delicatessen with my order, so the boy put the carton down on the counter and I fished a tip out of the jelly jar for him and by the time I got back the first two Giant batters had struck out and Ozzie Virgil was coming in to bat for Worthington. 'Louise,' Ed said to me, 'I think I will go out for a stroll, because for one thing I know goddam well what is about to transpire and I don't propose to sit here in this goddam broken-down chair in these dismal surroundings and watch these monkeys tie it up and then throw it away in the ninth, which they will unquestionably do.' Well, he got up from his chair, which isn't broken at all—we have very nice furniture—and tightened his necktie and Virgil lifted an easy fly to right, which Crandall went for. Crandall is not really an outfielder, Dr. Link, but Andy Pafko was out with an injury. 'The outfielder will drop the ball, Louise,' Ed said to me, 'but do not be deceived, Louise, my dear darling wife, do not be deceived.' Then he started for the door and caught sight of the beer bottles sticking out of the carton and so help me God it was Knickerbocker beer, which of course I never allow in the house on account of the violent way my husband feels about the little man. Well, Ed's face got absolutely livid with rage and guess what he did, Doctor."

"I'm afraid you'll have to tell me. Briefly."

"He grabbed an opener and flipped the cap off one of the bottles, then he started to sing the music they play for the little man, and Ed turned the bottle upside down and went marching all around the apartment with this crazy look in his eyes and imitating the man by raising his knees very high, like a drum majorette, with the beer spilling out all over everything—my new slipcovers, the rug, he even poured some beer on me. It was a print dress. It was just horrible. I was so frightened, Doctor. I couldn't even scream. Then Ed threw the empty bottle clear across the room at the TV set, but he didn't hit it, luckily. He never can hit anything when he's really sore, and then he stamped out of the apartment still raising his knees high like the little man and slammed the door. And believe it or not, what he had predicted was absolutely right. Crandall had dropped the ball in the middle of all this confusion. Then Lockman singled and Trowbridge walked Danny O'Connell and that loaded the bases, then Willie singled, bringing in two. Of course, I could hardly look, because I was so worried about my husband, and I took my sopping dress off and while I was going around with a wet rag trying to get the worst of it off the furniture, Thomson singled, and then Spencer and then Mueller, and so it was all tied up—a bran-new ball game, just the way Ed said it would be. He really doesn't have to look any more, he knows the Giants so well. And of course I knew they were going to lose the game, otherwise Ed wouldn't have stalked out of the apartment, and they did. The Braves picked up two in the ninth."

Mrs. Mooney opened her handbag and took out a handkerchief. Dr. Link hoped this did not presage tears. The narrative that he had just listened to had held his attention without in any way clarifying his thoughts. He was always grateful when a patient steered clear of the weird tangle of internal organs that made the human body so perplexing and hateful, but in this instance he felt as confused and dispirited as though she had told a long, dull tale of gastrointestinal malfunction. He had never watched a ball game in his life, and the formula of this woman's anguish did not appear, offhand, to be a simple one.

After a moment or two he said, "Mrs. Mooney, I take it you have come here to find out whether your husband is disturbed mentally, and it is very important, of course, that you should know. We can rule out the episode of the carbon paper—I feel sure it was a practical joke, at your expense. The violent profanity is significant, though not conclusive. I can't make a judgment without seeing the patient. You must get him to pay me a visit. If he needs psychiatric help, the sooner we know the better. From your account, I think perhaps he is just suffering, as many of us do these days, from emotional fatigue. The question here, medically, is the actual intensity of these attacks—I mean, we all have our petty irritations in this world; it's only when our responses are unusually strong that it indicates anything serious."

"Petty irritations?" said Mrs. Mooney incredulously. "The Giants?"

Dr. Link rose, as a signal that the interview was over. His estimate of Edward Mooney's condition was, as events were to show, wide of the mark. The episode of the carbon paper, which he dismissed summarily, was the clue, and he had failed to seize it. No practical joke had been involved (Mooney was no joker), and the paper had, in fact, picked up the seventh inning. Doctors, of course, are fallible. Link's unfamiliarity with the baseball scene was crippling: he failed to perceive that a personal identification with the New York Giants, which in tens of thousands of individuals is merely partial and unwholesome, in Edward Mooney was complete. It would be unfair to hold Dr. Link accountable for this error. The heat was intense—it was a ninety-seven-degree afternoon. As he stood up, a wave of dizziness lapped him, and he placed one hand on the desk to steady himself and closed his eyes momentarily.

"It's not just profanity, either," continued Mrs. Mooney, who did not understand that she was supposed to go. "Ed is blasphemous also. He doesn't only hate Rigney, he can't stand Billy Graham, either."

Dr. Link, in his despair, remained standing.

"You remember that time Billy Graham was in the Yankee Stadium —I think it was the night Nixon was there, too—and there was a man who pretended he was an usher and took up a collection, and they arrested him with the money—four hundred and ninety-one dollars?"

The doctor nodded impatiently.

"Ed says there's no such thing as sin, that's why he can't stand this Graham. Well, a couple of days later the papers printed a story about how Graham went to see the thief, to offer to forgive him. 'I forgive you,' he said. 'This experience should drive you back to God.' And the thief replied, 'I'm in enough trouble already.' Well, you should have heard Ed when he read that. He let out a whoop and threw the newspaper at the ceiling and then he started laughing, and he laughed in this wild sort of a way until I just couldn't stay in the apartment. Do you believe in sin, Doctor?"

Dr. Link walked to the air conditioner and put it back on COOL. Then he returned and stood in front of his patient. Warm as a rose, he thought. Mixed up as a . . . "My dear Mrs. Mooney," he said, "I believe in healing the sick, and I must see your husband. I can't do anything on the strength of these—these isolated episodes that you have related."

Mrs. Mooney nodded. She seemed spent by her recital. The doctor looked exhausted, too. Mrs. Mooney rose, dusted herself off, and started slowly and sadly for the door. "He won't come, Doctor. Ed isn't going to come here. If I should suggest it, he would go higher than a kite. He would start swearing and it would be as bad as ever. He uses terrible words. I've never heard some of them anywhere else. He used one on the telephone the other day and I had to remind him that a person can get arrested. A person can, can't you?"

"I really don't know," said Dr. Link feebly.

"Goodbye," she said, turning to face him as she squeezed the doorknob. The doctor studied her with a look that was both compassionate and curious.

"What channel did you say all this happens on?" he asked.

"Eleven."

After she was gone, Dr. Link tore a sheet of paper from a memo pad, wrote "11" on it, and tucked it in his pocket. Then he drew it out again hastily and added, "Gablonski."

Less than a week after this visit, Louise Mooney's fears were confirmed. She was home, fixing dinner; the phone rang and it was the police. Ed had been arrested for creating a disturbance in the subway. He had been taken first to a precinct station, then to a hospital for observation. The shock was so great, Louise felt it hardly at all. She simply felt numb all over, numb and full of grim resolution. By pulling every string at her command, and with Dr. Link's help, she managed to get her husband shifted to a hospital near where they lived.

Ed Mooney's mental condition soon proved to be the least of his troubles. Not even money was his chief trouble, although it was serious. The affair in the subway hadn't amounted to much—merely a few offensive remarks evoked by the text of a shampoo ad that happened to be right in front of him as he clung to his strap. But in the hospital a routine physical examination showed him to be suffering from an astounding complexity of diseases and disorders. The body, as we know, contains four fluids—blood, phlegm, choler, and melancholy. In Mooney, these had become so mingled as to produce a morbid state, so adulterated with the vapors of disappointment and defeat as to produce a fatal toxicity. It was here that Dr. Link took hold. He broke the news to Louise that Ed could not possibly live more than a few days.

Louise collapsed under this news, then quickly recovered and went to work with admirable vigor and courage. She borrowed two hundred dollars from the best-heeled of her many friends, took out a loan on her car, sold the one decent piece of jewelry she owned, and with this fund at her disposal got Mooney moved to a private room with a view. "Ed is going to have the best," she kept telling herself. She determined to dismiss money from her mind for the moment, and she succeeded. Day and night, almost continuously, Louise stayed with her husband in his room in the hospital. She considered renting a TV for the room, but the Giants were out of town, so she just brought her portable radio and they listened to the games through the long hot afternoons and sorrowful evenings. Under heavy sedation, Ed's vocabulary remained imaginative and lively, but it was pitched in a low key and was not bothersome. He died with Louise at his side during the ninth inning of a twi-night game with the Dodgers, just as Rhodes, hitting for Grissom, struck out looking at the 2-2 pitch.

Three days later, after a stopover in the neighborhood funeral home, Ed Mooney, who was without sin, entered the kingdom of heaven. To his immense surprise and amusement, he discovered that to get there you had to climb a short flight of stairs—seven steps, the same number used by Knickerbocker beer. Ed went up clowning all the way. It was a Saturday afternoon, between innings, and he could hear the music of the commercial. Ed and the little man climbed their stairs together, each his own peculiar flight, each to his own odd destination, each in his own strange world. They reached the top together: there wasn't a fraction of a second's difference in their times.

Late that same afternoon, Louise Mooney sat alone in her living room. The strain she had been under had drained some of the color from her face, but she was an attractive little widow as she sat in repose, staring at the unlighted television screen while her mind darted in and out of the shadow of unpaid hospital bills and funeral expenses. On Monday morning she would start looking for a job. She regretted nothing. "I would play it the same way if I had it to do again," she said, half aloud.

It was peaceful in the room without TV—an unwonted peace, a muggy, brooding afternoon in August. She found herself savoring the new-found tranquillity of bereavement. Ed had left an indelible mark on every familiar object in the room, and it was as though he were sitting there with her. The Giants had returned from their tour; their presence in the room was strong, too. Around five thirty, the phone rang; it was Ellie Snider, Louise's closest friend. Ellie and Sam had been wonderful through it all.

"I hesitated to call, Louise," said Ellie in a voice that sounded to Louise unnaturally tense. "But I just had to. I hope this isn't a bad moment, or anything?"

"No, certainly not, Ellie. I'm all right."

"I figured maybe you didn't have TV on—I mean, on account of being bereaved."

"That's correct, it's not on. It wouldn't be decent, Ellie. But what's the matter?"

"Listen, Louise, I don't know how to say this, and you're not going to believe it anyway, but it's true, so help me."

"What is true? You mean they beat Philadelphia?"

"Well, no, they didn't win, exactly. But that's not it, Louise. That's not what I'm talking about."

"Well, what *are* you talking about?"

"The money draw. Ed won the Giant draw. I just saw it myself. You're going to get a phone call, Louise, and I just wanted to warn you so it won't come as too much of a shock on top of everything else."

For a moment Louise Mooney sat impassively, holding the receiver.

Then she said, "Well, you couldn't have seen it right, Ellie. There is something fishy about it. Ed never would have signed his name to one of those Knickerbocker ballots, you know that. It's impossible."

"Ed didn't, but Sam signed Ed's name. I think he was a little high when he did it, but I'm not complaining. Sam and I loved Ed, Louise, and ever since he got sick Sam has been drinking more than usual, and of course he knew you were stony broke with all the extra expenses and everything and I guess he thought it would be O.K. under the circumstances, Louise. It's not really like forgery. Anyway, he was over to the Freedonia bar the other night—I believe actually it was the very night Ed passed on—and Sam wrote Ed's name and address on a ballot and dropped it in. Honestly, Louise, I'm so upset by all this I just can't—"

"Ellie," said Louise, "the draw is based on the number of runs scored, isn't it?"

"Of course it is. *You* know that. The winner gets a hundred dollars a run."

"Well, Ellie?"

"You're not going to believe this, Louise. Did you see any of the game at all—I mean, did you catch an inning toward the beginning? Or has your set been off the entire time."

"The entire time. Please tell me, Ellie. How much did Ed win?"

"Well, the Phils scored two in the third, four in the sixth, and two in the ninth, so when the Giants came to bat in the ninth inning, naturally it was eight-nothing. You know how they always wait till the game is more than half over, Louise, before they start anything? I think that's what made Ed so sick."

"Please tell me the final score, Ellie."

"I am. That's just what I'm telling you. Eddie Bressoud led off and went for the first pitch and it was a beautiful double. He came into second standing up. That brought Valmy Thomas up and Rigney called him back and put Gail Harris in to hit for him."

"Ed wouldn't have liked that," said Louise softly.

"I know it. But this is one time where Rigney was right. Harris looked at the first one, then he looked at the second one, then Roberts threw him a ball, then he fouled one back, and then he lined one up the middle, scoring Bressoud."

"That brings Worthington up?"

"That's right, Louise."

"And Jablonski goes in to hit for him?"

"That's right. Jabbo knocked one into the upper stands, a two-run homer, so it's eight to three, and the top of the order."

"Who came in to pitch for the Phils? Farrell?"

"That's right, Louise. So Lockman is up—"

"With the outfield shaded to the right?"

"Yes. Whitey singled. Then Danny O'Connell got him to second on a real deep sacrifice fly taken by Repulski. And then, Louise, there were back-to-back homers by Willie and Bobby Thomson."

"That's funny," said Louise, "I wouldn't expect back-to-back homers when it's only one away."

"I know," replied Ellie thoughtfully. "I had the same reaction myself. But that's what happened."

"It's eight to six, isn't it, Ellie?"

"Yes."

"I suppose they got Spencer for the second out?"

"Yes, they did. But it was close. He went for the two-one pitch and lined one out between Solly Hemus and Ed Bouchee, and the ball looked so good they tried to stretch it to a double and Spencer got tagged out sliding into second, but it was close and Rigney comes stalking out to protest the call and there is a dickens of a rhubarb out around second base."

"Then what happened?"

"The Phils took Farrell out and Jim Hearn came in to relieve him. Ozzie Virgil singled, and then Bressoud walloped one and it was bye bye baby."

"That ties it up, Ellie. I suppose the next batter flied out?"

"That's correct, Louise. A little pop-up by Harris over by first base."

"Hold the phone a minute, Ellie. I want to get my cigarettes." Louise Mooney set the receiver down daintily. She walked slowly across the room, found a pack of Pall Malls, and walked slowly back. Placing a cigarette cautiously between her lips, she picked up the phone again. "Ellie?" she said. "What do you think I should do?"

"Do? What do you mean, Louise?"

"All this money—you know perfectly well where it comes from."

"Sure. From Knickerbocker beer."

"You know how Ed felt."

"But Louise, Ed is—" Ellie checked herself. "Louise, you haven't even let me tell you about the extra inning."

"Just tell me how many runs Philadelphia got, please, Ellie," said Louise.

"Three."

"And then the Giants went out in one-two-three order?"

"Yes. So it was an eleven-to-eight ball game. That's nineteen hundred dollars, Louise. Golly, if you had had Blue Cross, *too . . .*"

"Ellie!" shouted Louise. "Stop it!" She slammed the receiver down on its cradle.

Slowly she detached a match from the paper matchbook she held in her hand. As she struck it, she could see the familiar face of Russ Hodges as she and Ed had watched him so many times, lighting his cigarette for

Pall Mall—his close-set eyes, his pleasant expression, the shirt Ed hated so. And for the first time since her husband's death, Louise Mooney felt the crushing weight of her loss and realized that she would never again be sitting with Ed in this beloved room, the two of them together, through the long, unhappy, predictable innings of play. The Giants are such a wonderful club, she thought—men like Mays, Antonelli, Spencer, Sauer —nothing wrong with them except that they don't win games. Sort of like Ed himself, so kind and gentle and concerned about the world, yet so ineffectual. A picture of San Francisco flashed into her head—she could get a little apartment there, brush up on her typing, find a job. Putting out her cigarette, she flung herself headlong onto the couch, her body racked with the sobbing that gave her for the first time a measure of relief. She lay there quite a while after it was over, until it was time to get up and fix herself the light supper that she would eat alone. She allowed the phone to ring five times before she walked over, picked up the receiver, and hopefully said, "Hello?"

DISTURBERS OF THE PEACE

The cows lie sweetly by the pond,
    At ease, at peace (except for flies);
The glassy morning waves its wand
    And bids the summer day arise.

Arise, O pesky day, arise!
    The peaceful cow, with flies to bother,
The dog his worms, the hen her lice,
    And Man—Man his eternal brother.

DEFINITIONS

COMMUTER

Commuter—one who spends his life
    In riding to and from his wife;
A man who shaves and takes a train
    And then rides back to shave again.

CRITIC

The critic leaves at curtain fall
    To find, in starting to review it,
He scarcely saw the play at all
    For watching his reaction to it.

PORTRAIT

He goes his way with a too cautious stride
That checks him safe just short of every goal;
Seeks not conclusions lest they try his pride,
Claims not fair booty lest it glut his soul.
If it be love, he finds it unrequited,
And seasons it with sadness to the taste;
If it be fame, he finds his name is slighted,
And turns his luck aside in conscious haste.
Frustration tickles his most plaintive strings
And satisfies his bent for somber living;
He daubs with mystery the obvious things,
And holds fulfillment off—always contriving
From life (held very gingerly) to press
The fine musk odor of unhappiness.

THE PASSING OF ALPHEUS W. HALLIDAY

(A December Tale)

Old Mr. Halliday, year upon year,
Showed small zest for the season of cheer.
At Santa's name, at holly's mention,
He sank in coils of apprehension.
A selfish man in his way of living,
He had no talent for gifts and giving;
The Yule, with its jumble of thistles and figs,
Was a lonely time in his bachelor digs.
Shopping for mistletoe, tinsel, and tree,
Alpheus Halliday still could foresee
Sitting in solitude, feet by the fire,
Opening things that he didn't desire.

*(He determines to correct this and give himself a walloping
present.)*

One grim noon, on his way to Saks,
Halliday halted, wheeled in his tracks,
Returned to the office, went up in the lift,
And ordered Miss Forbush wrapped as a gift.
Little Miss Forbush, out of Accounting,
Wrapped and sent (with his spirits mounting),
Sweet little Forbush, tidy and teeming,
Wreathed in the light of an old man's dreaming.

*(She is delivered to his home by United Parcel Service and placed
under the tree.)*

When Halliday wakened on Christmas morn,
He felt at peace and as though reborn.
The window was frosted, the gray clouds drifting,
A heavenly light, and the soft snow sifting.
He shaved and dressed and descended the stair
To see if old Santa had really been there.
Joyous and eager, he knelt at the tree,
Untied the red ribbon, and set his gift free.
He smoothened Miss Forbush and straightened her hair,
Then settled himself in his favorite chair.
Breathless with happiness, Halliday saw
That his gift to himself was a gift without flaw,
And though it was patently fraught with symbols,

It wasn't a thing you could buy at Gimbel's.

(She was something, all right.)

All the long morning, under the tree,
She lay there as quiet as quiet could be,
And there was a quality quite serene
About this relaxed and irregular scene.
There was never a hint of play or tussle;
Neither one of them moved a muscle.
The room had a clarity, cool and nice,
As though the two figures were sculptured in ice.

(I wish I had a photograph of it.)

All the long morning, in grateful surmise,
Alpheus Halliday studied his prize.
He seemed to be tracing, in Forbush's trance,
Patterns of loveliness, strains of the dance;
He seemed to be dreaming and tending the fires
Of old and, I trust, imprecise desires.
He seemed to be seeking to capture again
Certain lost fragrances, woods after rain.

(Miss Forbush very sensibly turns into barley sugar.)

At noon, ere either one had stirred,
A timely miracle occurred:
In silence and with gentle grace
She shed her mortal carapace;
Her form, her face, her eyes, her hair
Were barley sugar now for fair,
And though it seem to you incredible,
Miss Forbush . . . well, was fully edible.

(Halliday is well known for his sweet tooth.)

Stiffly but hungrily, Halliday rose,
Picked up Miss Forbush, and sampled her toes.
Here was the answer to all his vague wishes:
Little Miss Forbush was simply delicious.
Anxious to linger, yet hot to devour,
He ate his way onward, hour after hour.
The window was frosted, the gray clouds drifting,
A heavenly light, and the soft snow sifting.
Just as he finished her brow and her hair,
Old Mr. Halliday died in his chair.
Too much free sugar and time that's been spended—

Halliday's life was most tranquilly ended.
Perfect his passing as sweet was his tooth,
He died from an overindulgence in youth.

(Let us not judge him too harshly in this season of mercy and forgiveness.)

ABERCROMBIE'S DEEP-TANGLED
WILDWOOD

(A Vision of Happy Hours in the Great Outdoors,
After Reading the Latest A. & F. Catalogue)

The time is ripe, my love, for play,
    And stainless is the sky;
The woods are calling us away,
    And well equipped go I.

So step into my weldwood pram
    And seize the jointed oar;
In Thermo-Jug you'll find the jam,
    In Arga-Chest the boar.

Elastic-knit and buckle-free,
    We'll haunt the fields of fun;
Put on the kapok vest with me,
    And oil the Aqua-Gun.

There's fascinating sport ahead
    And many a lightweight thrill,
And Sturmey-Archer's dyna-bed
    Beneath the repellent hill.

With Coolapak and Broil-o-Kart
    And folding family grate,
We'll moccaround and kummapart
    Early, my love, and late.

In matching Lastex bra, my sweet,
    You'll dive into the river,
With rubber frogfins on your feet
    And arrows in your quiver.

A small electric megaphone
    Will amplify your guile,
And both our voices will be thrown
    Many a woodland mile.

I'll pack the old mint-julep set
    And ride to bag the bear,

A windproof ashtray in my kit
    And silver in my hair.

In terry cloth and karakul
    We'll haunt the fields of fun,
And thou beside the canvas pool,
    Wading, when day is done.

Let all our joys be monogrammed
    And all our boats inflated,
Let oxen on the spit be rammed
    And every check postdated.

There's fascinating sport ahead,
    And zippers to be zipped,
And, Love, it's like I've always said:
    You've got to go equipped.

IN CHARLIE'S BAR

ADELBURG, England (UPI)—Charlie's Bar at the Brudunell Hotel refused to serve Miss Jane Waterfield because she was wearing a mod costume that violated the bar's rule against showing belly buttons.—*The Times*

"Miss Waterfield, Miss Waterfield,
   What'll it be today?
The usual? The usual?
   That's all ye need to say.

"Miss Waterfield, Miss Waterfield!
   What do mine eyes behold?
What is that darling circle there?
   What's that adorable fold?

"Miss Waterfield, Miss Waterfield,
   What in the name of God
Has brought ye here to Charlie's Bar
   In clothes so utterly mod?

"Miss Waterfield, Miss Waterfield,
   We're plain as English mutton,
And yet we have our rules, my girl:
   No ale for a belly button.

"Miss Waterfield, Miss Waterfield,
   I fear ye must be going;
We cater to the middle class
   Whose middle isn't showing."

THE RED COW IS DEAD

Isle of Wight (AP)—Sir Hanson Rowbotham's favorite Red Polled cow is dead. Grazing in the lush pastures of the Wellow Farm, she was bitten on the udder by an adder.
—*The Herald Tribune*

Toll the bell, fellow,
This is a sad day at Wellow:
Sir Hanson's cow is dead,
His red cow,
Bitten on the udder by an adder.

Spread the bad news! What is more sudden,
What sadder than udder stung by adder?
He's never been madder, Sir Hanson Rowbotham.

The Red Polled cow is dead.
The grass was lush at very last,
And the snake (a low sneak)
Passed, hissed,
Struck.

Now a shadow goes across the meadow,
Wellow lies fallow.
The red cow is dead, and the stories go round.
"Bit in the teat by a dog in a fit."
"A serpent took Sir Hanson's cow—
A terrible loss, a king's ransom."

A blight has hit Wight:
The lush grass, the forked lash, the quick gash
Of adder, torn bleeding udder,
The cow laid low,
The polled cow dead, the bell not yet tolled
(A sad day at Wellow),
Sir Hanson's cow,
Never again to freshen, never again
Bellow with passion—
A ruminant in death's covenant,
Smitten, bitten, gone.
Toll the bell, young fellow!

FASHIONS IN DOGS

An Airedale, erect beside the chauffeur of a Rolls-Royce,
Often gives you the impression he's there from choice.

In town, the Great Dane
Is kept by the insane.

Today the Boxer
Is fashionable and snappy;
But I never saw a Boxer
Who looked thoroughly happy.

The Scotty's a stoic,
He's gay and he's mad;
His pace is a snail trot,
His harness is plaid.
I once had a bitch,
Semi-invalid, crazy:
There ne'er was a Scotch girl
Quite like Daisy.

Pekes
Are biological freaks.
They have no snout
And their eyes come out.
Ladies choose 'm
To clutch to their bosom.
A Pekinese would gladly fight a wolf or a cougar
But is usually owned by a Mrs. Applegate Krueger.

Cockers are perfect for Elizabeth Barrett Browning,
Or to carry home a package from the A&P without clowning.

The wire-haired fox
Is hard on socks
With or without clocks.

The smooth-haired variety
Has practically vanished from nice society,
And it certainly does irk us

That you never see one except when you go to the circus.

The dachshund's affectionate,
He wants to wed with you:
Lie down to sleep,
And he's in bed with you.
Sit in a chair,
He's there.
Depart,
You break his heart.

My Christmas will be a whole lot wetter and merrier
If somebody sends me a six-weeks-old Boston terrier.

Sealyhams have square sterns and cute faces
Like toy dogs you see at Macy's.
But the Sealyham, while droll in appearance,
Has no clearance.

Chows come in black, and chows come in red;
They could come in bright green, I wouldn't turn my head.
The roof of their mouth is supposed to be blue,
Which is one of those things that might easily be true.

To us it has never seemed exactly pleasant
To see a beautiful setter on East Fifty-seventh Street looking for a
    woodcock or a pheasant.

German shepherds are useful for leading the blind,
And for biting burglars and Consolidated Edison men in the behind.

Lots of people have a rug.
Very few have a pug.

MUCH ADO ABOUT PLENTY

(A street in the Matanuska Valley, Alaska.
Enter colonists and attendants.)

FIRST PIONEER: Four changes of the
    moon have not improved
The sad condition of our new estate:
Our roads not built, our floors un-
    carpeted,
Laxity rife among our senators,
Our children poxed and ailing.
SECOND PIONEER: He speaks truth.
Through this adventure, are we all
    agreed,
Incompetence creeps like an asp.
SERVANT: Let's blow, then!
FIRST PIONEER: Hold your tongue!
    Leave mutiny to your betters!
SECOND PIONEER: Things go from bad
    to worse. This very morn,
Fresh from the warming show'r,
    I did essay
To stem the faucet's flow, my bath
    being o'er,
Forthwith did twist and turn the
    cursèd thing—
SERVANT: Twisted it clockwise, too—
    I witnessed all . . .
SECOND PIONEER: And though I shut
    the valve as it should go,
Still did the water gush and drip,
    playing
A rib-a-dib upon the tiles.
FIRST PIONEER: Jerry-plumbing!
My home's the same. The windows
    stick. Handiwork
Of the CCC. And through the bare
    glass panes,
Uneased by gentle drape or dotted
    swiss,

Glares the Alaska sun.

SECOND PIONEER: Let's write Hop-
kins!

FOOL: Oh, sir, would'st like my cap to
scribble on?

FIRST PIONEER: Psst! Who comes
here?

(Enter a trouble shooter.)

SECOND PIONEER: An emissary from
the law, no doubt,

Come to inform us of our great good
luck.

Come on, let's pull his leg!

TROUBLE SHOOTER: Good morrow,
sweet settlers!

Sweet settlers, good morrow! What
seems to be the trouble?

SECOND PIONEER: Look in the bath-
room!

FOOL: Trouble, trouble,

Boil and bubble.

Those on relief-O

May well beef-O.

Beevo bivo bum,

Ibitty bibitty sibitty sock,

The water runneth in the bowls

When all the cocks are shut!

FIRST PIONEER: The fool, for all the
lightness of his tongue,

Shows forth our plight. We are not
happy here.

This is the nub of our complaint, my
lord:

Things that were promised us have
not been done.

TROUBLE SHOOTER: Anything you
could put your finger on?

FIRST PIONEER: Yes. All in good time.
First, sir, you must know

How dear to all our hearts our old
homes were.

Hast ever seen the moon adrift i' the
sky

Pouring her golden gift upon the
night

Till meadow, copse, stream, and the
    town's white steeple
Shine in her praise, make earth a
    paradise?
Hast seen that selfsame orb, stem-
    ming the blue
Of heav'n, plunge sudden down be-
    hind a cloud,
Blot out all lovely shapes, the earth
    grown dark?
So lost our hearts their light, when
    that our homes
Were given to the dust, and we
    came here
To try frontiers of freedom with our
    friends,
Looking upon this arctic, ominous
    soil,
Drear as a henyard on an August
    noon.
FOOL: Similes! Who'll buy my similes?
    Zzzzzzz.
FIRST PIONEER: Picture our present
    plight, weeks having passed,
No schools, roads still unbuilt, houses
    of logs,
Victuals so ill-prepared that when
    we sup
Our gorge doth rise. Radios mute.
    And in the bath
A faulty tap, with some great val-
    vular weakness,
Which, like a leaky heart, doth ever
    sap
What small remaining strength we
    call our own.
SECOND PIONEER: At the store they
    want ten cents for a Tootsie Roll,
The retail price, plus freight!
TROUBLE SHOOTER: I little dreamed,
My friends, that things had come
    to such a pretty pass.
A WOMAN: Is dinner ready yet?
FIRST PIONEER: No.
SERVANT: No, not yet.

WOMAN: Twelve o' the clock! My
    belly croaks and groans,
Yet none in all the Conservation
    Corps
Has raised a finger to prepare our
    meal.
Look you for trouble? How can we
    pioneer
On empty stomachs?
SERVANT: Let's picket the store.
FOOL: I know a merrier trick. Let's
    pitch some quoits!
If the steak's not toward, let's to-
    ward the stake!
SECOND PIONEER: Good!
CHORUS: Quoits! Quoits! Good fool!
    Someone fetch everything.
TROUBLE SHOOTER: May I play too?
FIRST PIONEER: Why not? They're
    government horseshoes.
SERVANT: Send someone for the gam-
    ing things, direct.
PAGE: Here are some horseshoes. I got
    'em off a horse.
SECOND PIONEER: Let's go.
TROUBLE SHOOTER: Oke.
FOOL: With a heigh-ho,
The wind and the rain.
So bless us while we take our
    pleasure
In this economy of leisure.

*(They pitch horseshoes. A freight
train pulls in, and members of the CCC
begin unloading prefabricated refrigerators.)*

FIN DE SAISON—PALM BEACH

(Special to Almost Any Metropolitan Daily)

PALM BEACH, FLA., March 31.—The marriage of Nancy Ann Bloodgood, daughter of Mr. and Mrs. Willis Fernandez Peel of Point Watchout, who have been spending the month as guests of the Parker Travises in their oceanfront villa, will take place in St. Thomas's on Labor Day, it was announced here today by Mrs. Trask Trap, sister of Mrs. Peel and formerly Lady Crenshaw Foote, who was divorced from Viscount Sanper Toogood in February, 1923, and has spent recent years in Paris and traveling with her stepson, Sir Horace Elsinore, Bart., F.T.B., L.L.U., C.C.C., P.W.A., a charter member of the Automobile Club of Rangoon. The church will be decorated with white chameleons and pink oleanders and the following will be bridesmaids: Nancy Van Der Weird, Nancy Fenner, Nancy Prankly, Nancy Toogood Wenn, Nancy DeLoncy Bloodgood Toogood, sister of the groom and first wife of young "Sandy" Elsinore, Nancy Fenner, and Lady Spurt Melton, sister of the bride's stepfather and known as a true dog lover. Mr. Fordyce is a student at Lawrenceville.

Mrs. James T. Afterguard entertained 1,425 friends at a luncheon in the patio of the Breaker Arms today. They discussed Lilyan Tashman's funeral.

Arrivals at Salle d'Armes Vince-on-Sea include Serge Aspirin and Madame Aspirinskaya, and Lord and Lady Herman Schulte, Lady Schulte being the daughter of Trelawney Alden and descended from a band of Seminole Indians on her mother's side. "The Indians started out on my father's side and changed over later after they got to know Dad," Lady Schulte likes to tell friends.

Rioting broke out in the cabaña of El Mintz last night when agitators representing the beach-umbrella hoisters overturned Mrs. Prudence Stickles and put a brick through her windshield.

John Peter Baggs, little son of Viscount and Slipshod Baggs, gave a sand-crab party for 123 little playmates in the basement of Bradley's yesterday. They played sand crab and won. Prizes went to Lloyd Demarest, Allan Nuts, and Percy Guam Stotzberry, 7, 8, and 9 respectively.

The temperature of the water was 72, air 73, at the Municipal Pier this morning. Rails and oils were off one to three points in sympathy with the beach-umbrella interests.

At the dog races the other night one of the dogs bit the following: Mrs. H. Fenner Euling, of Louisville, Ky., who wore a yellow and orange chiffon with velvet girdle and dropped shoulder line; Lady Polinor Sibitzky, of East Orange, in a crêpe frock of dusty pink with a wide girdle of rhinestones and oyster shells; Baron Temple Irksome, first son of Earl and Mother Dunruly, Castle Dunruly on the Llangollenen-Dunruly in County Limerick, Blasket Blasket. The Baron's town house is at 10 Downing Street and he is a member of the exclusive Turf and Surf Club. The dog was sent away for examination, but the veterinary reported that there was nothing much the matter with him. The Baron was given the Schick test.

The private railway car of Henry C. Rappleyea, maker of Chocolate Frenzies, was removed from the lawn opposite the Royal Poinciana Tuesday by nomads. Four people from West Palm Beach were injured in the disorders which followed.

Molton de Corbignac, former spermweight champion of the world, is seen daily at the cabaña of Aimee Tendril (Fritzi Ferguson).

Post-season pastimes and diversions of the winter colony include chewing the living bark off royal palms, caponizing mourning doves, and racing verbenas. The high neck is returning for beach wear, and one sees a great deal of fustian in large checks, often with a double row of silk fringe tied at the front where it is most needed.

A lady from the lower middle classes had the misfortune to be stung by a Portuguese Man o' War while in bathing this morning off the foot of Australian Avenue. She suffered severe pain in both "legs." The Florida press maintained a dignified silence.

Princess and Mr. Ludhvigk Dhavidh Pankhg gave a dinner dance at their villa, Casa Spray, last night for Strangler Lewis.

The cabaña of Lady Woolworth-Hollingwurth-Scheslinger has been condemned as a firetrap.

The Allsinger Kipps have left for Bar Harbor with a small party of friends on the Kippses' ice yacht Thermidor for the smelting. Many amusing parties have been scheduled during their stay "down east," and while there they will dare each other to hold their tongues against the cold runners.

Loch Ness is closed for the season.

The Rimpools have closed their villa and taken an umbrella on the Municipal Beach.

Your correspondent, who is down here in connection with a CWA project for diverting the effluvia of the proletariat from Lake Worth, feels better already. But the lake still smells at twilight.

GROWING UP IN NEW CANAAN

"It belongs to some people named Spillway," said Mrs. White. "Mr. Spillway is a writer."

We were talking about a house that we were driving out to look at. Mrs. White and I often drive out and look at houses on Sunday afternoon, feeling that there is no more stimulating pastime than snooping through other people's homes and commenting on the thousand and one little objections that we find to living in them.

"Did Mr. Spillway tell you how to get to the house, or is he simply a writer?" I asked.

"I know how to find it," said Mrs. White. "It's three miles out of New Canaan on a road, and it has a concrete mixer in the front yard."

"And a family of wrens in the concrete mixer?" I added, enthusiastically. "Did you know that wrens only build in concrete mixers that face northeast? And six weeks after the first eggs have hatched, the mother wren is at it again and lays another clutch."

We drove on for a while in the silence that usually follows humorous or informative remarks of that sort, and I kept wondering what the Spillways were doing with a concrete mixer in the front yard. "What are the Spillways doing with a concrete mixer in the front yard?" I finally asked.

"They have been adding on to the house."

We turned left on what Mrs. White called the "road," and in the course of the afternoon did come upon the Spillway house; and there, just as stated, was the concrete mixer. It wasn't exactly *in* the front yard, the front yard being a thing of the past, having been absorbed by the contractor. There were some traces of yard left, notably a bush, but the main body of it had been removed. Inside the house a painter was at work painting a wall, even though it was Sunday.

"Where are the Spillways?" I asked him.

"They ain't here."

"It's their house, isn't it?"

"Sure, but they're living down the road in another house. They'll be here any moment, though. You can look around if you want."

We soon found ourselves prying happily into the various rooms of the Spillway house—both the old section and the new addition. It was indeed a fine place, and we were in the midst of panning it loudly to each other when we were joined by the owners themselves, Mr. and Mrs. Spillway, whom I liked instantly. Mr. Spillway had brought along a bottle of whiskey: he was holding it dreamily in his hand as though he had forgotten to put it down. He and I followed Mrs. White and Mrs. Spillway at a little distance as the four of us wandered about through the treacherous corridors and dank sunrooms. It soon became apparent to me that the addition to the house had been Mrs. Spillway's idea, and that it had been achieved in a devilish clever fashion by gouging out the land in the rear and throwing it to one side, against the garage. I noticed, as we strolled about, that Mr. Spillway looked at everything with a sort of reminiscent curiosity and affection, bestowing on rooms, walls, and alterations a glance such as one sometimes gives one's child in a moment of objectivity, when one wonders how it all came about anyway. Several times he stopped and stared into a fireplace or at a door, as though he had never seen it before; and once I caught him staring peacefully into space, as though gazing at something that *had* been.

"This is the studio," said Mrs. Spillway, up ahead, entering a long white room, "where Mr. Spillway will do his work. Unless, of course, we sell." She smiled back at us men.

Mr. Spillway was still regarding everything with the same quiet, curious amazement. "What did she just say?" he asked.

"Said this was where you'd work," I whispered.

"You know what that means, I guess," he said. "Means this is where I'll sit with a couple of cronies, and drink."

I nodded.

"We might have one now," he murmured sadly, recalling the bottle of whiskey he held in his hand.

"Let's," I said. And we sat down on some old planks and drank quietly. Through the new French doors we could see the destruction out back, where the contractor had scored a direct hit. A few small trees remained of what had once been a wood.

"See that out there?" said my host. "Used to be all covered with violets in the spring." His eye came to rest on a wheelbarrow heavily encrusted with mortar. The ladies had gone upstairs, and we could hear Mrs. Spillway telling Mrs. White about a new door that had been knocked through between rooms, to save a person from going out into the hall. "We used to have to go out into the hall," we heard her say, "and it was a perfect nuisance."

"Wasn't bad," said my host softly, to me. "I didn't mind going out into the hall. I sometimes *like* going out into the hall. Gives you a change of scene. You know?"

I nodded, and pointed to the whiskey. "We might have another."

"Let's," said my host. After a minute or two he turned to me solemnly. "Listen," he said. "Want some fun? Ask to see the furnace." Again I nodded my head. We rose and joined the ladies in a bathroom.

"I was wondering," I said to Mrs. Spillway, who was standing in the tub to make more room for the rest of us, "whether I might see the furnace."

She stepped quickly out of the tub, giving her husband a glance. "It's an oil burner. They're the most marvelous things! We can go down this way, through the studio." Mrs. Spillway led us down, and out into the ruined yard. "The furnace is in the garage," she explained. "They always put them away from the house, for safety. And I want to tell you something funny that has happened to this one while the work has been going on here this winter."

"Don't tell them!" put in Mr. Spillway. "Let 'em look."

We entered the garage. In one corner of the concrete floor was a large pit, about six feet square and six feet deep, full to the brim of water. Sticking up above the surface, its gauge awash, its copper pipes disappearing into the cool depths, was an oil burner.

"See it?" said Mr. Spillway, pointing.

For a while nobody said anything. It was a spectacle that one looked at, not talked about.

"How the deuce did it happen?" I finally asked, thinking that that might be the thing to say about a furnace that had foundered.

"Well," replied Mrs. Spillway, gaily, "when they built the pit, they left a hole down there so that the outlet pipe could be cleaned if it ever got clogged, and they forgot that water could come *in* when we changed the level of the yard. It's really a scream, isn't it? I called up the oil-burner people and they said water wouldn't hurt it any."

Long after the ladies had gone from the garage, Mr. Spillway and I lingered on in the pleasant dampness, gazing down amiably into the brown waters of the furnace hole. "Want to know something else funny?" said Mr. Spillway after a while. His face again wore that rapt air of affectionate search. "It's true about the water."

"What do you mean?" I asked.

"About the water not hurting it. I investigated for myself. You wouldn't believe it, but it's perfectly true that water doesn't hurt the goddam thing."

R. F. TWEEDLE D.

(The Author's on the Pumpkin and the Dough Is in the Bag)

In 1923, after an interval of unexplained good health, I married a woman of some refinement. She had hazel eyes and absolute pitch. I had long been a writer, and there seemed to be but one course open to us—agriculture. If, in the ensuing pages, I refer repeatedly to Pearl's despondency on the farm and her jealousy of the shoats, it is because she moves through my life like a clear stream of running water, activating the young corn and sealing the Mason jars. In the early morning, when I take my typewriter and my lantern to the barn and stand for a moment listening to the heavy breathing of the creatures in the stanchions and watching the hired man rehearsing his part in the next Little Theater production of *Candida,* there stands Pearl, bathed in new light, opening can after can of prepared shoat food. We buy this by the case direct from Charles. It costs nine dollars per case of twenty-four cans, or a little less than eighty-three cents a hundredweight. We mix it with anchovy paste and slaked lime in the proportion of one part fresh fruit lemonade (which we bring home from the Little Theater) to sixteen parts soy. The shoats love it, but we never give it to them: we prefer to eat it ourselves, as it saves dishwashing.

All the dishwashing at Book Farm is done by the county agent, who visits Pearl on fetid summer afternoons when the brooder stoves have gone out and she is warming the young pullets by holding her great bombazine skirt over them. Most of the time Pearl wears no skirt—just shorts and a fez. I wear orange slacks made of sailcloth, and a postman's hat. We always bathe nude in the drinking trough in the dairy, where the cold, clear water trickles in steadily like royalties from a good piece of nonfiction. There is no plumbing in our house and not the slightest advantage or convenience. I took the wainscoting down yesterday and re-hewed it along my own lines. You don't hear the word "re-hew" used much nowadays, but I always use it and so does Pearl. We got into a merry argument, after three Manhattans, as to whether the wainscoting was ready to be bred. Our neighbor, Mr. Enoch Galway, happened by and surprised us in the midst of this badinage and probably thought we were queer ones. Country folk have a solid worth, which is as purifying as a glass of milk.

I am a state-accredited veterinary, and in lambing time I sometimes go a week at a time without sleep, my eyes open as wide as teacups. Lambing, like any other farm operation, is largely a knack and is by no means as dangerous as it used to be. I usually take along a copy of *Life* to the lambing ground—which is in the bottomlands just this side of the stadium. There is something peaceful about the miracle of birth, and what the popular magazines don't know about it the ewe does, or thinks she does. Pearl is no help in lambing, but I leave the entire docking of the shoats' tails to her, as well as the laundering of the kilts; and to both these country chores she brings a kind of pagan excitement without which this rural existence would be a mere pause between two worlds. We made a profit on the sheep this year for the first time. I sold two of the rams to a circus for an animal act, and the government bought all the wool to stuff into the dikes along the Mississippi. I do not believe in flood control, however, nor do I derive any satisfaction except a financial one from the twenty-five-thousand-dollar-a-year income which we get from certain investments left us by Pearl's uncle, who made a fortune a generation ago by the old conventional corn-wheat-grass rotation.

The cows pay well, too. We never drink the milk, because that would mean washing the pail. Instead, we make it into clabber, and then the clabber is processed and becomes rubber, which we use for tractor tires. The tractor is invaluable to us in turning over the ground for the spring planting of fodder corn for the cows. Thus does nature pursue her inexorable cycle.

The years are a green parade with banners flying. Farming has its compensations and pays dividends in health and serenity—although the first five years we were here Pearl had shingles continuously and our doctor's bill ran well over four hundred dollars a month. I can always sell words, and it is the only crop I enjoy marketing. We grade and candle our words and store them in the root cellar. I have taught Pearl to save only the Latin roots and feed the others to the shoats, mixed with apple cores and middlings. Neither Pearl nor I knew what middlings were when we came here in 1923, and although she handles them every day, Pearl still doesn't know. But the serene mornings, the steady push of the year, nights compounded of mystery and good talk and cider in season, and the county agent out in the kitchen with the dirty dishes, these are what make life supportable to us and fascinating to hundreds of thousands of Americans who are aware that something rather odd is happening in this country but are not sure yet quite what it is.

THE GASTROPODS

(An answer to a hard question)

Q: I have an aquarium, and I got a snail for it because they told me it would keep the water clean, and the snail unexpectedly bore young, although it was in there all alone. I mean there weren't any other snails in there, only fish. How could it have young, very well?

A: The snail in your aquarium is a mollusk. It is quite likely an hermaphrodite, even though it came from a reputable department store. For being hermaphroditic, nobody can blame a snail. We cannot tell you everything we know about the gastropods because we know, possibly, more than is good for us. In the absence of specific information to the contrary, we would say that the snail in your aquarium had been going around a good deal with other snails before you got him (her). Some mollusks (not many) can have children merely by sitting around and thinking about it. Others can have children by living in a state of reciprocity with other hermaphrodites. Still others are like us, dioecious, possessed of only one sexual nature but thankful for small favors.

The shellfish and the snails are a great group, though it is a pose with many people to consider them dull. Usually the people who find mollusks dull are dull themselves. We have met mollusks in many parts of the world: in gardens in France, on the rocks at low tide on Long Island Sound, in household aquaria, on the sidewalks of suburban towns in the early mornings, in restaurants, and in forests. Everywhere we found them to be sensitive creatures, imaginative and possessed of a lively sense of earth's pleasant rhythm. Snails have a kind of nobility. Zoologists will tell you that they occupy, in the animal kingdom, a position of enviable isolation. They go their own way.

We can understand your curiosity about sex in snails. Mollusks are infinitely varied in their loves, their hates, and their predilections. They have a way of carrying out ideas they get in their head. They are far from cold, as many people suppose them; indeed, one of the most fascinating love stories we ever read was in the *Cambridge Natural History,* in which was described the tryst kept by a pair of snails on a garden wall. We have never forgotten the first sentence of that romantic and idyllic tale, nor have we forgotten the name of the snail, L. Maximus. The story started: "L. Maximus has been observed at midnight to ascend a wall or some perpendicular surface." It then went on to relate how, after some moments spent greeting each other, crawling round and round, the snails let themselves down on a little ladder of their own devising, and there, suspended in the air ten inches or so from the top of the wall, they found love.

Often very fecund, mollusks are rarely too busy to give attention to their children after birth, or to prepare for their coming. There is, in Algeria, a kind of mollusk whose young return for shelter to the body of their mother, somewhat in the manner of little kangaroos. There is, in the Philippines, a snail who is so solicitous for her expected babies that she goes to the trouble of climbing, with infinite pains and no little discomfort, to the top of a tall tree, and there deposits her eggs in a leaf, folding the leaf adroitly for protection. Another kind of mollusk, having laid her eggs upon a stone, amuses herself by arranging them like the petals of a rose, and hatches them by holding her foot on them. Mollusks tend to business.

Sometimes different species intermarry, but this is rare. The interesting point about it is that such unions generally take place when the air is heavily charged with electricity, as before a storm, or when great rains have made the earth wet. The Luxembourg Garden in Paris is a place snails go to for clandestine matches of this sort. H. Variabilis goes there, and Pisana. The moisture, the electricity, the fragrant loveliness of a Paris night, stir them strangely.

Probably, if you know so little of the eroticism of snails, you have not heard of the darts some of them carry—tiny daggers, hard and sharp, with which they prick each other for the excitement it affords. These darts are made of carbonate of lime. The Germans call them *Liebespfeil,* "love shaft." Many British mollusks are without them, but that's the way it goes.

We could tell much more. We could tell about mollusks that possess the curious property of laying their eggs on the outside of their own shell, and of the strange phenomenon of the Cephalopod, who, when he takes leave of his lady, leaves one of his arms with her, so that she may never lack for an embrace. But we feel we have answered your question.

THE WINGS OF ORVILLE

All through the courtship, the building of the nest, and even the incubation of the eggs, Orville had acted in what to the hen sparrow seemed a normal manner. He had been fairly attentive, too, as cockbirds go. The first indication Orville's wife had of any quirk in his nature came one morning when he turned up before breakfast carrying a ginger-ale bottle cap in his beak.

"I won't be home for lunch," he said. His mate looked at the bottle cap.

"What's that for?"

Orville tried to act preoccupied, but it wasn't a success. He knew he'd better make a direct answer. "Well," he said, "I'm going to fly to Hastings-upon-Hudson and back, carrying this bottle cap."

The hen looked at him. "What's the idea of carrying a bottle cap up the river and back?"

"It's a flight," replied Orville, importantly.

"What do you mean, it's a *flight?* How else would you get there if you didn't fly?"

"Well, this is different," said Orville. "I want to prove the practicability of a round-trip flight between Madison Square and Hastings-upon-Hudson carrying a bottle cap."

There wasn't anything she could say to that. Orville stayed around for a few minutes; then, after what seemed to his wife a great deal of unnecessary fluttering on the edge of the nest, he gripped the bottle cap firmly in his bill and departed. She noticed that he was flying faster than his usual gait and was keeping an unusually straight course. Dutifully she watched him out of sight. "He'll be all tuckered out when he gets back," she thought to herself.

Orville, as the hen sparrow had expected, was tired that evening; but he seemed pleased with the results of the day.

"How did it go?" asked his wife, after he had deposited the bottle cap on the base of the statue of Admiral Farragut.

"Fine," said Orville. "I ran into a little rain the other side of Yonkers, but kept right on into fair weather again. It was only bad once, when ice began to form on my wings."

His wife looked at him intently. "I don't believe for a minute," she said, "that any ice started to form on your wings."

"Yes, it did," replied Orville. "For a while there, it was nip and tuck."

He mooched about the nest for a while and went into a few details for the benefit of his three children.

The nest occupied by Orville's family was in a tree in Madison Square near the Farragut statue. It was no neater than most sparrows' nests and had been constructed eagerly of a wide variety of materials, including a kite string that hung down. One morning, a few days after the Hastings affair, Orville came to his wife with a question. "Are you through with that string?" he asked, nodding toward the trailing strand.

"Are you crazy?" she replied, sadly.

"I need it for something."

His wife gazed at him. "You're going to wreck the nest if you go pulling important strings out."

"I can get it out without hurting anything," said Orville. "I want it for a towline."

"A what?"

"Listen," said Orville, "I'm going to fly to 110th Street tomorrow, towing a wren."

The hen sparrow looked at him in disgust. "Where are you going to get a wren?"

"I can get a wren," he said, wisely. "It's all arranged. I'm going to tow it till we get up about three thousand feet, and then I'm going to cut the wren loose and it will glide down to a landing. I think I can prove the feasibility of towing a wren behind a sparrow."

Orville's wife did not say anything more. Grudgingly she helped him pull the kite string from the nest. Pretty strange doings, it seemed to her.

That evening Orville experimented alone with his string, tying it first to one foot and then the other. Next morning he was up at the crack of dawn and had the string all lashed to his right leg before breakfast. Putting in the half hitches had occasioned an immense lot of kicking around and had been fairly uncomfortable for the youngsters.

"For goodness' sake, Orville," said the hen sparrow, "can't you take it down to the ground and tie it on there?"

"Do me a favor," said Orville. "Put your finger on this knot while I draw it tight."

When the towline was arranged to his complete satisfaction, he flew down to the Square. There he immediately became the center of attention. His wife, noticing how other birds gathered around, was a bit piqued to see all this fuss made over Orville. Sparrows, she told herself, will gape at anything queer. She didn't believe that Orville had actually located a wren and was genuinely surprised when one showed up—a tiny brown bird, with sharp eyes and a long, excitable tail. Orville greeted the wren cordially, hopping briskly round and round dragging the line. When about fifty sparrows and pigeons had congregated, he took the wren to one side. "I don't want to take off," he said, "till we get a weather report."

The news that the flight was to be delayed pending a report on weather conditions increased the interest of the other birds, and one of them volunteered to fly up to Central Park and back to find out how things were. He was back in ten minutes and said the weather was clear. Orville, without any hesitation, motioned to the wren, who seized the towline in its beak, spread its wings rigidly, and waited. Then, at a signal from Orville, they both ran as fast as they could along the grass and jumped wildly into the air, Orville beating his wings hard. One foot, two feet, three feet off the ground they soared. Orville was working like a horse. He put everything he had into it, but soon it became clear that they hadn't enough altitude to clear a park bench that loomed up directly ahead—and the crash came. Orville landed with the string tangled in one wing, and the wren fell to the ground, stunned.

No further attempt to tow a wren was made that day. Orville felt sick, and so did the wren. The incident, however, was the talk of the Square, and the other birds were still discussing it when night fell. When Orville's wife settled herself on the roosting branch beside her mate for the twittering vespers, she turned to him and said, "I believe you could have made it, Orville, if that darn bench hadn't been there."

"Sure we could have."

"Are you going to try again tomorrow?" There was a note of expectation in her voice.

"Yes."

The hen sparrow settled herself comfortably beside him. He, if any sparrow could, would prove the feasibility of towing a wren. For a minute she roosted there, happily. Then, when Orville had dropped off to sleep, she stole quietly down to the kitchen and busied herself making two tiny sandwiches, which she tied up in wax paper.

"I'll give him these tomorrow," she murmured, "just before he takes off."

VI

THESE

CONQUERING

DAYS

EVER POPULAR AM I, MAMMOTH, WILT RESISTANT

(A Man, Having Lasted Fifteen Rounds with the Seed Catalogue, Finds His Life for a Brief Spell Perfect in Every Particular)

Ever popular am I, Mammoth, Wilt Resistant,
By far the best variety for forcing under glass,
I the Prolific, I the Tendergreen,
This is my golden moment, this is my finest hour.
Newly improved in color, sturdy, tall,
I, who was once so late, now Earliest of All;
Mine is the fruit unblemished, mine the Paramount flower.

Who are my friends and familiars, I the Contender?
Snowball Imperial, Crosby's Egyptian—I the free spender
    (Pkt. 15¢; ½ Oz. 40¢. A packet will sow 25 to 30 feet of row, an
    ounce about a hundred feet),
I, in this vernal deception, matchless pretender,
Crisp and delicious, deep, outstanding,
Vigorous, sweet,
Exceeding all others for canning and freezing,
Firm, attractive, common, sweet-scented,
Valiant, amazing, brilliant, productive,
Proven reliable, best for the garden
(And my soil friable).

Save me these conquering days, this moment of triumph!
Never shall beetle intrude, or the slightest unthriftiness.
Shall a man spoil his occasion, thinking of August?
No, I shall plant with assurance, dwell with perfection,
Live with my dream till that night in late summer when,
Down from her hole in the tree, the fastidious coon,
One with the shadows, knowing the pleasures of plunder,
Full of the evil of darkness, enters the rows while I sleep,
Takes all but five ears of the corn called Wonderful.

PASTURE MANAGEMENT

Down below the pasture pond,
    O'er the lovely lea,
I went spraying bushes
    With 2, 4-D.

(For young, susceptible annual weeds, apply one to two pints per acre.)

I had read my bulletins,
    I was in the know.
The two young heifers
    Came and watched the show.

(Along ditches and fence rows, use 2, 4-D when weeds are in a succulent stage. Won't harm livestock.)

Rank grew the pasture weeds,
    The thistle and the bay;
A quiet, still morning,
    A good time to spray.

(Control weeds the easy way with Agricultural Weed-No-More—not by chemical burn but by hormone action.)

Suddenly I looked and saw
    What my spray had found:
The wild, shy strawberry
    Was everywhere around.

(An alkyl ester of 2, 4-D is produced by reacting an alcohol with the raw 2, 4-D acid. The result is an oily liquid that sticks to weed leaves.)

What sort of madness,
    Little man, is this?
What sort of answer to
    The wild berry's kiss?

(Any 3- or 4-gallon garden pump-up sprayer can be used, after the

standard nozzle has been replaced with a new precision nozzle.)

It seemed to me incredible
    That I'd begun the day
By rendering inedible
    A meal that came my way.
All across the pasture in
    The strip I'd completed
Lay wild, ripe berries
    With hormones treated.

(The booklet gives you the complete story.)

I stared at the heifers,
    An idiot child;
I stared at the berries
    That I had defiled.
I stared at the lambkill,
    The juniper and bay.
I walked home slowly
    And put my pump away.
Weed-No-More, my lady,
    O weed no more today.

(Available in quarts, 1-gallon and 5-gallon cans, and 55-gallon drums.)

THE MISSTEP

Keepers at a London zoo have taught an orangutan to clean its
own cage, says the National Geographic Society.
                                                    —*The Times*

This is the way it starts, you know:
A first misstep in the long ago,
An Early She in the foul cave's gloom
Fumbles with twigs, and behold—a broom!
At first, the dimmest sort of revulsion;
Centuries later, a washing compulsion.
From jungle dark with fern and creeper
Up to the light of a Bissell's sweeper;
A fateful moment—Woman Emergent,
Sowing the seeds of a pink detergent.

Ponder your deed, O tidy ape!
There's no road back and no escape.
This single spark from your cloudy dome
Kindles the watchfires of The Home.
In one wild moment of feeling superior
You've opened the floodgates of The Interior.
And distant monks in a distant age
Will sigh when they think of the Early Cage.

INNERSPRING MATTRESSES

Americans have invented many undesirable things,
The most notable being mattresses with inner springs.

Developed on the principle that beds should be pliant,
Mattresses of today are no longer self-reliant.

They not only conform to the shape of *you*
But to the shape of a couple of other people, too.

You go to bed and you are true and straight;
You arise next morning and you are a figure eight.

You get into bed and turn on your belly
And discover you are suspended in guava jelly.

Your day may be done, with its troubles and toils,
But your night is beginning, with its series of coils.

I would rather go down in a storm off Hatt'ras
Than founder in bed on an innerspring mattress.

> I have slept, in my time, on all sorts of material,
> But an innerspring mattress is the most ethereal.
> I have slept on kapok, down, and floss,
> I have bedded on shavings and straw and moss,
> I've slept in gully and in savanna,
> In dried-up streams near Butte, Montana;
> I've slept quite prone in dark morasses,
> And bolt upright in history classes,
> On every kind of a mound and lump,
> In Louisville, Kentucky's, municipal dump;
> I've lain on hillocks, crests, and knolls,
> In cracks and crevices and in holes,
> In fields and sidings and in stables,
> In empty conference rooms, on tables,
> On flatbed presses and in tanneries,
> On old board floors, with mice, in granaries;
> I've slept in sand traps on green fairways,
> Reclined (with hostesses) on airways,

But though my dreams at times aborted,
My back and thighs were well supported.
I'll take any bed from saint or sinner
Provided it has no springs that are inner.

Love, you may bring me my cap and my nightie,
And trot out that slab of lignum vitae.

SURVIVAL THROUGH ADAPTATION

Scientists recently reported we Yankees possess the most powerful index fingers in the world. And to what do they attribute this digital superiority? You guessed it. The telephone dial!
—Stuffer with a bill from the New England Telephone Company.

How did the fiddler crab (the male),
Uca pugnax, acquire his outsize claw,
Picking his preposterous fights in muddy Lilliput
Among the stilts of mangrove in the vast
Intertidal zone, hurling his challenges,
Waving the enormous tiny disproportionate
Claw (which slowly grew by being waved), flashing
His semaphore across the stinking flats?
How? A matter of survival. The necessities of life.

And the frog, *Rana* (the male), with his notorious
Phallic thumb. Whence came this strange
    appendage?
Where else but from sheer necessity, to hold
His slippery mate for the exact, the correct
Performance of his offices.

And now I, Man (the male), most splendid
Of the Mammalia, *Homo sapiens,* longtime
Darling of the New England Telephone Company
With my enormous index finger, perfectly adapted
To my environment, I, endlessly phoning,
Hurling my challenges, quarreling, conducting
My courtships, picking my fights long distance
With this incredible index finger, the
Most powerful in the world. Now I, a New Englander,
Join the company of the immortals: the frog,
The crab, who slowly changed in subtle ways
In order to survive. I, too. Hey!
Cock-a-doodle-doo! Watch me dial!

APOSTROPHIC NOTES FROM
THE NEW-WORLD PHYSICS

The universe, according to Sir James Jeans, British scientist, is a system of waves. Space and time and the physical world of substances have no objective reality apart from the mental concepts of them that man creates with his mind. "Thus we can never know the essential nature of anything."

SWEET READER

Sweet reader, whom I've never seen,
    And who, thereby, is nonexistent,
To you my thoughts in space careen,
    This page not real, myself so distant!
    Substantial dear, all unperceived,
    For your reality I've grieved!
    And Sir James Jeans
    Knows what that means.

AH, LOVE

Ah, Love, my dearest and mine own,
    So sweetly tangible in pleasance,
How utterly am I alone—
    A widower, save in your presence;
    The while in space you undulate,
    Most cherished and unconscious mate!
    And Sir James Jeans
    Knows what that means.

GOOD SIR

Good sir who builded us the span
    That seems to bridge the Hudson River,
Suspending from Aldebaran
    My sometimes quite apparent flivver,
    Your postulates were ill-defined
    Did I not keep the bridge in mind!
    As Sir James Jeans
    Most certainly means.

MOST MERCIFUL GOD

Most merciful and loving God
 Who giveth us the will to wonder
If naught save where we tread is sod
 And naught save what we hear is thunder,
 I stoop upon this seeming knee
 In praise of things I know and see.
 For it is my essential nature
 To simulate a grateful creature.
 If Sir James Jeans
 Knows what that means.

THE SUPREMACY OF URUGUAY

Fifteen years after the peace had been made at Versailles, Uruguay came into possession of a very fine military secret. It was an invention, in effect so simple, in construction so cheap, that there was not the slightest doubt that it would enable Uruguay to subdue any or all of the other nations of the earth. Naturally the two or three statesmen who knew about it saw visions of aggrandizement; and although there was nothing in history to indicate that a large country was any happier than a small one, they were very anxious to get going.

The inventor of the device was a Montevideo hotel clerk named Martín Casablanca. He had got the idea for the thing during the 1933 mayoralty campaign in New York City, where he was attending a hotel-men's convention. One November evening, shortly before the election, he was wandering in the Broadway district and came upon a street rally. A platform had been erected on the marquee of one of the theaters, and in an interval between speeches a cold young man in an overcoat was sing-ing into a microphone. "Thanks," he crooned, "for all the lovely dee-light I found in your embrace. . . ." The inflection of the love words was that of a murmurous voice, but the volume of the amplified sound was enor-mous; it carried for blocks, deep into the ranks of the electorate. The Uruguayan paused. He was not unfamiliar with the delight of a love embrace, but in his experience it had been pitched lower—more inti-mate, concentrated. This sprawling, public sound had a curious effect on him. "And thanks for unforgettable nights I never can replace. . . ." People swayed against him. In the so bright corner in the too crowded press of bodies, the dominant and searching booming of the love singer struck sharp into him and he became for a few seconds, as he later realized, a loony man. The faces, the mask-faces, the chill air, the adver-tising lights, the steam rising from the jumbo cup of A&P Coffee high over Forty-seventh Street, these added to his enchantment and his un-balance. At any rate, when he left and walked away from Times Square and the great slimy sounds of the love embrace, this was the thought that was in his head:

If it unhinged me to hear such a soft crooning sound slightly am-plified, what might it not do to me to hear a far greater sound greatlier amplified?

Mr. Casablanca stopped. "Good Christ!" he whispered to himself; and his own whisper frightened him, as though it, too, had been amplified.

Chucking his convention, he sailed for Uruguay the following afternoon. Ten months later he had perfected and turned over to his government a war machine unique in military history—a radio-controlled plane carrying an electric phonograph with a retractable streamlined horn. Casablanca had got hold of Uruguay's loudest tenor and had recorded the bar of music he had heard in Times Square. "Thanks," screamed the tenor, "for unforgettable nights I never can replace. . . ." Casablanca prepared to step it up a hundred and fifty thousand times, and grooved the record so it would repeat the phrase endlessly. His theory was that a squadron of pilotless planes scattering this unendurable sound over foreign territories would immediately reduce the populace to insanity. Then Uruguay, at her leisure, could send in her armies, subdue the idiots, and annex the land. It was a most engaging prospect.

The world at this time was drifting rapidly into a nationalistic phase. The incredible cancers of the World War had been forgotten, armaments were being rebuilt, hate and fear sat in every citadel. The Geneva gesture had been prolonged, but only by dint of removing the seat of disarmament to a walled city on a neutral island and quartering the delegates in the waiting destroyers of their respective countries. The Congress of the United States had appropriated another hundred million dollars for her naval program; Germany had expelled the Jews and recast the steel of her helmets in a firmer mold; and the world was re-living the 1914 prologue. Uruguay waited till she thought the moment was at hand and then struck. Over the slumbrous hemispheres by night sped swift gleaming planes, and there fell upon all the world, except Uruguay, a sound the equal of which had never been heard on land or sea.

The effect was as Casablanca had predicted. In forty-eight hours the peoples were hopelessly mad, ravaged by an ineradicable noise, ears shattered, minds unseated. No defense had been possible because the minute anyone came within range of the sound, he lost his sanity and, being daft, proved ineffectual in a military way. After the planes had passed over, life went on much as before, except that it was more secure, sanity being gone. No one could hear anything except the noise in his own head. At the actual moment when people had been smitten with the noise, there had been, of course, some rather amusing incidents. A lady in West Philadelphia happened to be talking to her butcher on the phone. "Thanks," she had just said, "for taking back that tough steak yesterday. And thanks," she added, as the plane passed over, "for unforgettable nights I never can replace." Linotype operators in composing rooms chopped off in the middle of sentences, like the one who was setting a story about an admiral in San Pedro:

I am tremendously grateful to all the ladies of San Pedro for the wonderful hospitality they have shown the men of the fleet during our recent maneuvers and thanks for unforgettable nights I never can replace and thanks for unforgettable nights I nev-

To all appearances Uruguay's conquest of the earth was complete. There remained, of course, the formal occupation by her armed forces. That her troops, being in possession of all their faculties, could establish her supremacy among idiots, she never for a moment doubted. She assumed that with nothing but lunacy to combat, the occupation would be mildly stimulating and enjoyable. She supposed her crazy foes would do a few rather funny, picturesque things with their battleships and their tanks and then surrender. What she failed to anticipate was that her foes, being mad, had no intention of making war at all. The occupation proved bloodless and singularly unimpressive. A detachment of her troops landed in New York, for example, and took up quarters in the RKO Building, which was fairly empty at the time; and they were no more conspicuous around town than the Knights of Pythias. One of her battleships steamed for England, and the commanding officer grew so enraged when no hostile ship came out to engage him that he sent a wireless (which of course nobody in England heard): "Come on out, you yellow-bellied rats!"

It was the same story everywhere. Uruguay's supremacy was never challenged by her silly subjects, and she was very little noticed. Territorially her conquest was magnificent; politically it was a failure. The peoples of the world paid slight attention to the Uruguayans, and the Uruguayans, for their part, were bored by many of their territorials—in particular by the Lithuanians, whom they couldn't stand. Everywhere crazy people lived happily as children, in their heads the old refrain: "And thanks for unforgettable nights. . . ." Billions dwelt contentedly in a fool's paradise. The earth was bountiful, and there was peace and plenty. Uruguay gazed at her vast domain and saw the whole incident lacked authenticity.

It wasn't till years later, when the descendants of some early American idiots grew up and regained their senses, that there was a wholesale return of sanity to the world, land and sea forces were restored to fighting strength, and the avenging struggle was begun which eventually involved all the races of the earth, crushed Uruguay, and destroyed mankind without a trace.

ABOUT MYSELF

I am a man of medium height. I keep my records in a Weis Folder Re-order Number 8003. The unpaid balance of my estimated tax for the year 1945 is item 3 less the sum of items 4 and 5. My eyes are gray. My Selective Service order number is 10789. The serial number is T1654. I am in Class IV-A, and have been variously in Class 3-A, Class I-A(H), and Class 4-H. My social security number is 067-01-9841. I am married to U.S. Woman Number 067-01-9807. Her eyes are gray. This is not a joint declaration, nor is it made by an agent; therefore it need be signed only by me —and, as I said, I am a man of medium height.

I am the holder of a quit-claim deed recorded in Book 682, Page 501, in the county where I live. I hold Fire Insurance Policy Number 424747, continuing until the 23 day of October in the year nineteen hundred forty-five, at noon, and it is important that the written portions of all policies covering the same property read exactly alike. My cervical spine shows relatively good alignment with evidence of proliferative changes about the bodies consistent with early arthritis. (Essential clinical data: pain in neck radiating to mastoids and occipito-temporal region, not constant, moderately severe; patient in good general health and working.) My operator's licence is Number 16200. It expired December 31, 1943, more than a year ago, but I am still carrying it and it appears to be serving the purpose. I shall renew it when I get time. I have made, published, and declared my last will and testament, and it thereby revokes all other wills and codicils at any time heretofore made by me. I hold Basic A Mileage Ration 108950, O.P.A. Form R-525-C. The number of my car is 18-388. Tickets A-14 are valid through March 21st.

I was born in District Number 5903, New York State. My birth is registered in Volume 3/58 of the Department of Health. My father was a man of medium height. His telephone number was 484. My mother was a housewife. Her eyes were blue. Neither parent had a social security number and neither was secure socially. They drove to the depot behind an unnumbered horse.

I hold Individual Certificate Number 4320-209 with the Equitable Life Assurance Society, in which a corporation hereinafter called the employer has contracted to insure my life for the sum of two thousand dollars. My left front tire is Number 48KE8846, my right front tire is Number 63T6895. My rear tires are, from left to right, Number 6N4M5384 and Number A26E5806D. I brush my hair with Whiting-Adams Brush Number 010 and comb my hair with Pro-Phy-Lac-Tic Comb Number 1201. My shaving brush is sterilized. I take Pill Number

43934 after each meal and I can get more of them by calling ELdorado 5-6770. I spray my nose with De Vilbiss Atomizer Number 14. Sometimes I stop the pain with Squibb Pill, Control Number 3K49979 (aspirin). My wife (Number 067-01-9807) takes Pill Number 49345.

I hold War Ration Book 40289EW, from which have been torn Airplane Stamps Numbers 1, 2, and 3. I also hold Book 159378CD, from which have been torn Spare Number 2, Spare Number 37, and certain other coupons. My wife holds Book 40288EW and Book 159374CD. In accepting them, she recognized that they remained the property of the United States Government.

I have a black dog with cheeks of tan. Her number is 11032. It is an old number. I shall renew it when I get time. The analysis of her prepared food is guaranteed and is Case Number 1312. The ingredients are: Cereal Flaked feeds (from Corn, Rice, Bran, and Wheat), Meat Meal, Fish Liver and Glandular Meal, Soybean Oil Meal, Wheat Bran, Corn Germ Meal, 5% Kel-Centrate [containing Dried Skim Milk, Dehydrated Cheese, Vitamin B_1 (Thiamin), Flavin Concentrate, Carotene, Yeast, Vitamin A and D Feeding Oil (containing 3,000 U.S.P. units Vitamin A and 400 U.S.P. units Vitamin D per gram), Diastase (Enzyme), Wheat Germ Meal, Rice Polish Extract], 1½% Calcium Carbonate, .00037% Potassium Iodide, and ¼% Salt. She prefers offal.

When I finish what I am now writing it will be late in the day. It will be about half past five. I will then take up Purchase Order Number 245-9077-B-Final, which I received this morning from the Office of War Information and which covers the use of certain material they want to translate into a foreign language. Attached to the order are Standard Form Number 1034 (white) and three copies of Standard Form Number 1034a (yellow), also "Instructions for Preparation of Voucher by Vendor and Example of Prepared Voucher." The Appropriation Symbol of the Purchase Order is 1153700.001-501. The requisition number is B-827. The allotment is X5-207.1-R2-11. Voucher shall be prepared in ink, indelible pencil, or typewriter. For a while I will be vendor preparing voucher. Later on, when my head gets bad and the pain radiates, I will be voucher preparing vendor. I see that there is a list of twenty-one instructions which I will be following. Number One on the list is: "Name of payor agency as shown in the block 'appropriation symbol and title' on the upper left-hand corner of the Purchase Order." Number Five on the list is: "Vendor's personal account or invoice number," but whether that means Order Number 245-9077-B-Final, or Requisition B-827, or Allotment X5-207.1-R2-11, or Appropriation Symbol 1153700.001-501, I do not know, nor will I know later on in the evening after several hours of meditation, nor will I be able to find out by consulting Woman 067-01-9807, who is no better at filling out forms than I am, nor after taking Pill Number 43934, which tends merely to make me drowsy.

I owe a letter to Corporal 32413654, Hq and Hq Sq., VII AAF S.C., APO 953, c/o PM San Francisco, Calif., thanking him for the necktie he sent me at Christmas. In 1918 I was a private in the Army. My number was 4,345,016. I was a boy of medium height. I had light hair. I had no absences from duty under G.O. 31, 1912, or G.O. 45, 1914. The number of that war was Number One.

DAYLIGHT AND DARKNESS

Up early this day, trying to decide whether or not to bequeath my brain to my alma mater, which is making a collection of such stuff. It struck me as odd that the decision will have to be made by the brain itself and that no other part of me—a foot or a gallbladder—can be in on the matter, although all are, in a way, concerned. My head is small and I fear that my brain may suffer by comparison if arranged on a shelf with others. Spent part of the morning composing an inscription to go with my brain, but all I got was this:

> Observe, quick friend, this quiet noodle,
> This kit removed from its caboodle.
> Here sits a brain at last unhinged,
> On which too many thoughts impinged.

Spent the rest of the morning studying the crisis in the newspapers and watching apple-fall and leaf-fall in my city backyard, where nature is cleverly boxed and has therefore an appearance of special value, as of a jewel so precious that it must always be suitably contained. The day was clear, with a gentle wind, and the small leaves descended singly and serenely, except now and then when a breeze entered and caused a momentary rain of leaves—what one weather prophet on the radio calls "inner mitten" showers. A school of fish paraded slowly counterclockwise in the fountain, and on the wall above me hung seed pods of the polygonum vine. My complaint about the crisis is not that it is so appalling but that it is so trivial. The consequences of the atomic cataclysm that are being relentlessly published seem mild alongside the burning loveliness of a fall morning, or the flash of a south-bound bird, or the wry smell of chrysanthemums in the air. I examined everything said yesterday in the council chambers of the mighty and could find not a single idea that was not trifling, not a noble word of any caliber, not one unhurried observation or natural thought. The newspaper headline prophesying darkness is less moving than the pool of daylight that overflows upon it from the window, illuminating it. The light of day—so hard at times to see, so convincing when seen.

THE AGE OF DUST

On a sunny morning last week, I went out and put up a swing for a little girl, age three, under an apple tree—the tree being much older than the girl, the sky being blue, the clouds white. I pushed the little girl for a few minutes, then returned to the house and settled down to an article on death dust, or radiological warfare, in the July *Bulletin of the Atomic Scientists,* Volume VI, No. 7.

The article ended on a note of disappointment. "The area that can be poisoned with the fission products available to us today is disappointingly small; it amounts to not more than two or three major cities per month." At first glance, the sentence sounded satirical, but a rereading convinced me that the scientist's disappointment was real enough—that it had the purity of detachment. The world of the child in the swing (the trip to the blue sky and back again) seemed, as I studied the ABC of death dust, more and more a dream world with no true relation to things as they are or to the real world of discouragement over the slow rate of the disappearance of cities.

Probably the scientist-author of the death-dust article, if he were revising his literary labors with a critical eye, would change the wording of that queer sentence. But the fact is, the sentence got written and published. The terror of the atom age is not the violence of the new power but the speed of man's adjustment to it—the speed of his acceptance. Already, bombproofing is on approximately the same level as mothproofing. Two or three major cities per month isn't much of an area, but it is a start. To the purity of science (which hopes to enlarge the area) there seems to be no corresponding purity of political thought, never the same detachment. We sorely need, from a delegate in the Security Council, a statement as detached in its way as the statement of the scientist on death dust. This delegate (and it makes no difference what nation he draws his pay from) must be a man who has not adjusted to the age of dust. He must be a person who still dwells in the mysterious dream world of swings, and little girls in swings. He must be more than a good chess player studying the future; he must be a memoirist remembering the past.

I couldn't seem to separate the little girl from radiological warfare —she seemed to belong with it, although inhabiting another sphere. The article kept getting back to her. "This is a novel type of warfare, in that it produces no destruction, except to life." The weapon, said the author, can be regarded as a horrid one, or, on the other hand, it "can be regarded as a remarkably humane one. In a sense, it gives each member of the target population [including each little girl] a choice of whether he will live or die." It turns out that the way to live—if that be your choice—is to leave the city as soon as the dust arrives, holding "a folded, dampened handkerchief" over your nose and mouth. I went outdoors again to push the swing some more for the little girl, who is always forgetting her handkerchief. At lunch I watched her try to fold her napkin. It seemed to take forever.

As I lay in bed that night, thinking of cities and target populations, I saw the child again. This time she was with the other little girls in the subway. When the train got to 242nd Street, which is as far as it goes into unreality, the children got off. They started to walk slowly north. Each child had a handkerchief, and every handkerchief was properly mois-tened and folded neatly—the way it said in the story.

I SPY

The games of little boys at play,
    I-Spy and Run-Sheep-Run,
Trouble the street the livelong day
    And all is for the fun.

And when the lads grow up in fame
    And make a subtler noise,
They plot and plan and play the game
    They played when they were boys.

In darkling street they seek and hide,
    The game grows wild and drunken;
They spy upon the other side,
    Keep secrets in a punkin.

So let us think on little boys
    And love-of-fire that lingers,
On simple and remembered joys
    And how to burn the fingers.

The street grows dark, the night is hot,
    And so the game has trended.
Whether we know it, lads, or not,
    The game is nearly ended.

Run, sheep, run! Run wild and fast—
    A game to end the day with.
Look at the sky! A fire at last
    Too big for boys to play with!

WINDOW LEDGE
IN THE ATOM AGE

I have a bowl of paper whites,
    Of paper-white narcissus;
Their fragrance my whole soul delights,
    They smell delissus.
      (They grow in pebbles in the sun
      And each is like a star.)

I sit and scan the news hard by
    My paper-white narcissus;
I read how fast a plane can fly,
    Against my wissus.
      (The course of speed is almost run,
      We know not where we are.)

They grow in pebbles in the sun,
    My beautiful narcissus,
Casting their subtle shade upon
    Tropical fissus.
      (No movement mars each tiny star;
      Speed has been left behind.)

I'd gladly trade the latest thing
    For paper-white narcissus;
Science, upon its airfoil wing,
    Now seems pernissus.
      (Who was it said to travel far
      Might dissipate the mind?)

I love this day, this hour, this room,
    This motionless narcissus;
I love the stillness of the home,
    I love the missus.
      (She grows in pebbles in my sun
      And she is like a star.)

And though the modern world be through
    With paper-white narcissus,
I shall arise and I shall do
    The breakfast dissus.
     (The tranquil heart may yet outrun
      The rocket and the car.)

SONG OF THE QUEEN BEE

"The breeding of the bee," says a United States Department of
Agriculture bulletin on artificial insemination, "has always
been handicapped by the fact that the queen mates in the air
with whatever drone she encounters."

When the air is wine and the wind is free
And the morning sits on the lovely lea
And sunlight ripples on every tree,
Then love-in-air is the thing for me—
    I'm a bee,
    I'm a ravishing, rollicking, young queen bee,
    That's me.

I wish to state that I think it's great,
Oh, it's simply rare in the upper air,
    It's the place to pair
    With a bee.
Let old geneticists plot and plan,
They're stuffy people, to a man;
Let gossips whisper behind their fan.
    (Oh, she *does*?
    Buzz, buzz, buzz!)
My nuptial flight is sheer delight;
I'm a giddy girl who likes to swirl,
    To fly and soar
    And fly some more,
      I'm a bee.
And I wish to state that I'll *always* mate
    With whatever drone I encounter.

There's a kind of a wild and glad elation
In the natural way of insemination;
Who thinks that love is a handicap
Is a fuddydud and a common sap,
For I am a queen and I am a bee,
I'm devil-may-care and I'm fancy-free,
The test tube doesn't appeal to me,
    Not me,
    I'm a bee.

And I'm here to state that I'll *always* mate
    With whatever drone I encounter.

Let mares and cows, by calculating,
Improve themselves with loveless mating,
Let groundlings breed in the modern fashion,
I'll stick to the air and the grand old passion;
I may be small and I'm just a bee
But I *won't* have Science improving *me,*
    Not me,
    I'm a bee.
On a day that's fair with a wind that's free,
Any old drone is the lad for me.

I have no flair for love *moderne,*
It's far too studied, far too stern,
I'm just a bee—I'm wild, I'm free,
    That's me.
I can't afford to be too choosy;
In every queen there's a touch of floozy,
    And it's simply rare
    In the upper air
    And I wish to state
    That I'll *always* mate
With whatever drone I encounter.

Man is a fool for the latest movement,
He broods and broods on race improvement;
What boots it to improve a bee
If it means the end of ecstasy?
    (He ought to be there
    On a day that's fair,
    Oh, it's simply rare
      For a bee.)
Man's so wise he is growing foolish,
Some of his schemes are downright ghoulish;
He owns a bomb that'll end creation
And he wants to change the sex relation,
He thinks that love is a handicap,
He's a fuddydud, he's a simple sap;
Man is a meddler, man's a boob,
He looks for love in the depths of a tube,
His restless mind is forever ranging,
He thinks he's advancing as long as he's changing,

He cracks the atom, he racks his skull,
Man is meddlesome, man is dull,
Man is busy instead of idle,
Man is alarmingly suicidal,
    Me, I'm a bee.

I am a bee and I simply love it,
I am a bee and I'm darned glad of it,
I am a bee, I know about love:
You go upstairs, you go above,
You do not pause to dine or sup,
The sky won't wait—it's a long trip up;
You rise, you soar, you take the blue,
It's you and me, kid, me and you,
It's everything, it's the nearest drone,
It's never a thing that you find alone.
    I'm a bee,
    I'm free.

If any old farmer can keep and hive me,
Then any old drone may catch and wive me;
I'm sorry for creatures who cannot pair
On a gorgeous day in the upper air,
I'm sorry for cows who have to boast
Of affairs they've had by parcel post,
I'm sorry for man with his plots and guile,
His test-tube manner, his test-tube smile;
I'll multiply and I'll increase
As I always have—by mere caprice;
For I am a queen and I am a bee,
I'm devil-may-care and I'm fancy-free,
Love-in-air is the thing for me,
    Oh, it's simply *rare*
    In the beautiful air,
      And I wish to state
      That I'll *always* mate
With whatever drone I encounter.

TWO LETTERS, BOTH OPEN

New York, N.Y.
12 April 1951

The American Society for the Prevention of Cruelty to Animals
York Avenue and East 92nd Street
New York 28, N.Y.

Dear Sirs:

I have your letter, undated, saying that I am harboring an unlicensed dog in violation of the law. If by "harboring" you mean getting up two or three times every night to pull Minnie's blanket up over her, I am harboring a dog all right. The blanket keeps slipping off. I suppose you are wondering by now why I don't get her a sweater instead. That's a joke on you. She has a knitted sweater, but she doesn't like to wear it for sleeping; her legs are so short they work out of a sweater and her toenails get caught in the mesh, and this disturbs her rest. If Minnie doesn't get her rest, she feels it right away. I do myself, and of course with this night duty of mine, the way the blanket slips and all, I haven't had any real rest in years. Minnie is twelve.

In spite of what your inspector reported, she has a license. She is licensed in the State of Maine as an unspayed bitch, or what is more commonly called an "unspaded" bitch. She wears her metal license tag but I must say I don't particularly care for it, as it is in the shape of a hydrant, which seems to me a feeble gag, besides being pointless in the case of a female. It is hard to believe that any state in the Union would circulate a gag like that and make people pay money for it, but Maine is always thinking of something. Maine puts up roadside crosses along the highways to mark the spots where people have lost their lives in motor accidents, so the highways are beginning to take on the appearance of a cemetery, and motoring in Maine has become a solemn experience, when one thinks mostly about death. I was driving along a road near Kittery the other day thinking about death and all of a sudden I heard the spring peepers. That changed me right away and I suddenly thought about life. It was the nicest feeling.

You asked about Minnie's name, sex, breed, and phone number. She doesn't answer the phone. She is a dachshund and can't reach it, but she wouldn't answer it even if she could, as she has no interest in outside calls. I did have a dachshund once, a male, who was interested in the telephone, and who got a great many calls, but Fred was an exceptional dog (his name was Fred) and I can't think of anything offhand that he *wasn't* interested in. The telephone was only one of a thousand things. He loved life—that is, he loved life if by "life" you mean "trouble," and of course the phone is almost synonymous with trouble. Minnie loves life, too, but her idea of life is a warm bed, preferably with an electric pad, and a friend in bed with her, and plenty of shut-eye, night and day. She's almost twelve. I guess I've already mentioned that. I got her from Dr. Clarence Little in 1939. He was using dachshunds in his cancer-research experiments (that was before Winchell was running the thing) and he had a couple of extra puppies, so I wheedled Minnie out of him. She later had puppies by her own father, at Dr. Little's request. What do you think about *that* for a scandal? I know what Fred thought about it. He was some put out.

Sincerely yours,
E. B. White

New York, N.Y.
12 April 1951

Collector of Internal Revenue
Divisional Office
Bangor, Maine

Dear Sir:

I have your notice about a payment of two hundred and some-odd dollars that you say is owing on my 1948 income tax. You say a warrant has been issued for the seizure and sale of my place in Maine, but I don't know as you realize how awkward that would be right at this time, because in the same mail I also received a notice from the Society for the Prevention of Cruelty to Animals here in New York taking me to task for harboring an unlicensed dog in my apartment, and I have written them saying that Minnie is licensed in Maine, but if you seize and sell my place, it is going to make me look pretty silly with the Society, isn't it? Why would I license a dog in Maine, they will say, if I don't live there? I think it is a fair question. I have written the Society, but purposely did not mention the warrant of seizure and sale. I didn't want to mix them up, and it might have sounded like just some sort of cock and bull story. I have always paid my taxes promptly, and the Society would think I was kidding, or something.

Anyway, the way the situation shapes up is this: I am being accused in New York State of dodging my dog tax, and accused in Maine of being behind in my federal tax, and I believe I'm going to have to rearrange my life somehow or other so that everything can be brought together, all in one state, maybe Delaware or some state like that, as it is too confusing for everybody this way. Minnie, who is very sensitive to my moods, knows there is something wrong and that I feel terrible. And now *she* feels terrible. The other day it was the funniest thing, I was packing a suitcase for a trip home to Maine, and the suitcase was lying open on the floor and when I wasn't looking she went and got in and lay down. Don't you think that was cute?

If you seize the place, there are a couple of things I ought to explain. At the head of the kitchen stairs you will find an awfully queer boxlike thing. I don't want you to get a false idea about it, as it looks like a coffin, only it has a partition inside, and two small doors on one side. I don't suppose there is another box like it in the entire world. I built it myself. I made it many years ago as a dormitory for two snug-haired dachshunds, both of whom suffered from night chill. Night chill is the most prevalent dachshund disorder, if you have never had one. Both these dogs, as a matter of fact, had rheumatoid tendencies, as well as a great many other tendencies, specially Fred. He's dead, damn it. I would feel a lot better this morning if I could just see Fred's face, as he would know instantly that I was in trouble with the authorities and would be all over the place, hamming it up. He was something.

About the tax money, it was an oversight, or mixup. Your notice says that the "first notice" was sent last summer. I think that is correct, but when it arrived I didn't know what it meant as I am no mind reader. It was cryptic. So I sent it to a lawyer, fool-fashion, and asked him if *he* knew what it meant. I asked him if it was a tax bill and shouldn't I pay it, and he wrote back and said, No, no, no, no, it isn't a tax bill. He advised me to wait till I got a bill, and then pay it. Well, that was all right, but I was building a small henhouse at the time, and when I get building something with my own hands I lose all sense of time and place. I don't even show up for meals. Give me some tools and some second-handed lumber and I get completely absorbed in what I am doing. The first thing I knew, the summer was gone, and the fall was gone, and it was winter. The lawyer must have been building something, too, because I never heard another word from him.

To make a long story short, I am sorry about this nonpayment, but you've got to see the whole picture to understand it, got to see my side of it. Of course I will forward the money if you haven't seized and sold the place in the meantime. If you have, there are a couple of other things on my mind. In the barn, at the far end of the tieups, there is a goose sitting on eggs. She is a young goose and I hope you can manage everything so as not to disturb her until she has brought off her goslings. I'll give you one, if you want. Or would they belong to the federal government anyway, even though the eggs were laid before the notice was mailed? The cold frames are ready, and pretty soon you ought to transplant the young broccoli and tomato plants and my wife's petunias from the flats in the kitchen into the frames, to harden them. Fred's grave is down in the alder thicket beyond the dump. You have to go down there every once in a while and straighten the headstone, which is nothing but a couple of old bricks that came out of a chimney. Fred was restless, and his headstone is the same way—doesn't stay quiet. You have to keep at it.

I am sore about your note, which didn't seem friendly. I am a friendly taxpayer and do not think the government should take a threatening tone, at least until we have exchanged a couple of letters kicking the thing around. Then it might be all right to talk about selling the place, if I proved stubborn. I showed the lawyer your notice about the warrant of seizure and sale, and do you know what he said? He said, "Oh, that doesn't mean anything, it's just a form." What a crazy way to look at a piece of plain English. I honestly worry about lawyers. They never write plain English themselves, and when you give them a bit of plain English to read, they say, "Don't worry, it doesn't mean anything." They're hopeless, don't you think they are? To me a word is a word, and I wouldn't dream of writing anything like "I am going to get out a warrant to seize and sell your place" unless I meant it, and I can't believe that my government would either.

The best way to get into the house is through the woodshed, as there is an old crocus sack nailed on the bottom step and you can wipe the mud off on it. Also, when you go in through the woodshed, you land in the back kitchen right next to the cooky jar with Mrs. Freethy's cookies. Help yourself, they're wonderful.

Sincerely yours,
E. B. White

HEAVIER THAN AIR

The first time I ever saw a large, heavy airplane drop swiftly out of the sky for a landing, I thought the maneuver had an element of madness in it. I haven't changed my opinion much in thirty years. During that time, to be sure, a great many planes have dropped down and landed successfully, and the feat is now generally considered to be practicable, even natural. Anyone who, like me, professes to find something implausible in it is himself thought to be mad. The other morning, after the Convair dived into the East River, an official of the Civil Aeronautics Board said that the plane was "on course and every circumstance was normal"—a true statement, aeronautically speaking. It was one of those statements, though, that illuminate the new normalcy, and it encouraged me to examine the affair more closely, to see how far the world has drifted toward accepting the miraculous as the commonplace. Put yourself, for a moment, at the Convair's controls and let us take a look at this day's normalcy. The speed of a Convair, approaching an airport, is about a hundred and forty miles an hour, or better than two miles a minute. I don't know the weight of the plane, but let us say that it is heavier than a grand piano. There are passengers aboard. The morning is dark, drizzly. The skies they are ashen and sober. You are in the overcast. Below, visibility is half a mile. (A few minutes ago it was a mile, but things have changed rather suddenly.) If your forward speed is two miles per minute and you can see half a mile after you get out of the overcast, that means you'll be able to see what you're in for in the next fifteen seconds. At the proper moment, you break out of the overcast and, if you have normal curiosity, you look around to see what's cooking. What you see, of course, is Queens —an awful shock at any time, and on this day of rain, smoke, and shifting winds a truly staggering shock. You are close to earth now, doing two miles a minute, every circumstance is normal, and you have a fifteen-second spread between what you *can* see and what you can't. What you hope to see, of course, is Runway 22 rising gently to kiss your wheels, but, as the passenger from Bath so aptly put it, "When I felt water splashing over my feet, I knew it wasn't an airport."

Airplane design has, it seems to me, been fairly static, and designers have docilely accepted the fixed-wing plane as the sensible and natural form. Improvements have been made in it, safety devices have been added, and strict rules govern its flight. But I'd like to see plane designers start playing with ideas less rigid than those that now absorb their fancy. The curse of flight is speed. Or, rather, the curse of flight is that no opportunity exists for dawdling. And so weather is still an enormous factor in air travel. Planes encountering fog are diverted to other airports and set their passengers down hundreds of miles from where they want to be. In very bad weather, planes are not permitted to leave the ground at all. There are still plenty of people who refuse to fly simply because they don't like to proceed at two miles a minute through thick conditions. Before flight becomes what it ought to be, a new sort of plane will have to be created—perhaps a cross between a helicopter and a fixed-wing machine. Its virtue will be that its power can be used either to propel it rapidly forward or to sustain it vertically. So armed, this airplane will be able to face bad weather with equanimity, and when a pall of melancholy hangs over Queens, this plane will be seen creeping slowly down through the overcast and making a painstaking inspection of Runway 22, instead of coming in like a grand piano.

The above remarks on flying drew a fine letter from a TWA captain. His observations reveal a man so well adjusted to this life that they deserve being published. It isn't every day that you encounter a serene personality, either on land or in the sky. The captain did not take exception to my rather sour view of heavier-than-air flight; he merely testified that the acceptance of aerial hazards made him feel "time-fitted" to his profession and "apt to our second of history." (Stylist as well as pilot.)

> To move at a high rate of speed; to feel less secure the closer I come to earth and man; to be able to look ahead with some certainty for 15 seconds; —these factors characterize life in the world today. For most people this constitutes a constant hardship, including a rebellion and fretfulness against life. I suspect that by not merely accepting an unforeseeable future, but by building it into my life, I may come closer to living a "normal" 20th century life than those who must still struggle against it.

Well, there you have birdman and philosopher rolled into one—the contemplative pilot, full of semicolons, perfectly sympathetic to modern urgencies, a man with a built-in unforeseeable future who has surrendered himself to his speedy century as proudly and passionately as a bride to her lover. He would be my choice of a pilot if I had to go anywhere by air. Happily, however, my own mind is quiet today, and I shall travel afoot in the Park, time-fitted to the life of a weekly hack, unfretful, grateful for the next fifteen seconds.

The mental poise of this airline pilot in the middle of difficult flight shows man's spirit maintaining a small but significant lead over his instrument panel. My own earth-bound life, I realize, is schizophrenic. Half the time I feel blissfully wedded to the modern scene, in love with its every mood, amused by its every joke, imperturbable in the face of its threat, bent on enjoying it to the hilt. The other half of the time I am the fusspot moralist, suspicious of all progress, resentful of change, determined to right wrongs, correct injustices, and save the world even if I have to blow it to pieces in the process. These two characters war incessantly in me, and probably in most men. First one is on top, then the other —body and soul always ravaged by the internal slugging match. I envy Captain X, who has come out a whole man instead of a divided one and who is at peace with his environment. I envy all who fly with him through the great sky.

DEAR MR. ⑈0 2 14⑈ 1063⑈ ⑈0 2⑈ 10 7 30⑈8⑈

My bank, which I have forgotten the name of in the excitement of the moment, sent me a warning the other day. It was headed: "An important notice to all our checking account customers." The burden of this communication was that I would no longer be allowed to write checks that did not bear the special series of magnetic ink numbers along the base.

My bank said the Federal Reserve System had notified them that it will not accept for processing any checks that don't show these knobby little digits. For example, I would no longer be free to write a check on a blank form, because it would lack a certain magnetism that computers insist on.

I first encountered these spooky numbers a few years back and took a dislike to them. They looked like numbers that had been run over by a dump truck or that had developed rheumatoid arthritis and their joints had swollen. But I kept my mouth shut, as they seemed to be doing me no harm.

Now, however, it appears that we are all going to knuckle under to the machines that admire these numbers. We must all forego the pleasure and convenience of writing a check on an ordinary, nonmagnetic piece of paper. My signature used to be enough to prod my bank into dispatching some of my money to some deserving individual or firm. Not any more.

This, I think, is a defeat for all—a surrender. In order to accommodate the Federal Reserve System, we are asked to put ourselves out.

The notice I received says that if I try to palm off a check that lacks the magnetic ink numbers, the check cannot be processed without "delay, extra handling charges, and possible embarrassment." I embarrass easily—it doesn't take much, really—and naturally I am eager to learn what form this embarrassment will take if I should decide to write a check using the old blank form that has proved so convenient, for I don't know how many decades, on those occasions when one is stuck without his checkbook or enough lettuce to carry the day.

"The tremendous increase in the use of checks," writes my bank, warming to its subject, "made it necessary for the Federal Reserve to establish a completely computerized operation for processing all checks from all banks. Their computer can function only when proper magnetic numbers are used."

Well, I can believe that last part, about the computer requiring a special diet of malformed numbers; but I am suspicious of that first statement, about how the Federal Reserve would have been unable to carry on unless it went completely over to machines. I suspect that the Federal Reserve simply found machines handy and adventurous. But suppose we had had, in this country, a tremendous increase in the use of checks before anybody had got round to inventing the computer—what would have happened then? Am I expected to believe that the Federal Reserve and all its members would have thrown in the sponge?

I know banks better than that. Banks love money and are not easily deflected from the delicious act of accumulating it. Love would have found a way. Checks would have cleared.

I'm not against machines, as are some people who feel that the computer is leading us back into the jungle. I rather *like* machines, particularly the eggbeater, which is the highest point the machine has yet reached. I'm against machines only when the convenience they afford to some people is regarded as more important than the inconvenience they cause to all.

In short, I don't think computers should wear the pants or make the decisions. They are deficient in humor, they are not intuitive, and they are not aware of the imponderables. The men who feed them seem to believe that everything is made out of ponderables, which isn't the case. I read a poem once that a computer had written, but didn't care much for it. It seemed to me I could write a better one myself, if I were to put my mind to it.

And now I must look around for a blank check. It's time I found out what form my new embarrassment is going to take. First, though, I'll have to remember the name of my bank. It'll come to me, if I sit here long enough. Oddly enough, the warning notice I received contained no signature. Imagine a bank forgetting to sign its name!

MRS. WIENCKUS

The Newark police arrested a very interesting woman the other day—a Mrs. Sophie Wienckus—and she is now on probation after being arraigned as disorderly. Mrs. Wienckus interests me because her "disorderliness" was simply her capacity to live a far more self-contained life than most of us can manage. The police complained that she was asleep in two empty cartons in a hallway. This was her preferred method of bedding down. All the clothes she possessed she had on—several layers of coats and sweaters. On her person were bankbooks showing that she was ahead of the game to the amount of $19,799.09. She was a working woman —a domestic—and, on the evidence, a thrifty one. Her fault, the Court held, was that she lacked a habitation.

"Why didn't you rent a room?" asked the magistrate. But he should have added parenthetically "(and the coat hangers in the closet and the cord that pulls the light and the dish that holds the soap and the mirror that conceals the cabinet where lives the aspirin that kills the pain)." Why didn't you rent a room "(with the rug that collects the dirt and the vacuum that sucks the dirt and the man that fixes the vacuum and the fringe that adorns the shade that dims the lamp and the desk that holds the bill for the installment on the television set that tells of the wars)?" I feel that the magistrate oversimplified his question.

Mrs. Wienckus may be disorderly, but one pauses to wonder where the essential disorder really lies. All of us are instructed to seek hallways these days (except schoolchildren, who crawl under the desks), and it was in a hallway that they found Mrs. Wienckus, all compact. I read recently that the only hope of avoiding inflation is through ever increasing production of goods. This to me is always a terrifying conception of the social order—a theory of the good life through accumulation of objects. I lean toward the order of Mrs. Wienckus, who has eliminated everything except what she can conveniently carry, whose financial position is solid, and who can smile at Rufus Rastus Johnson Brown. I salute a woman whose affairs are in such excellent order in a world untidy beyond all belief.

THE FAMILY THAT DWELT APART

On a small, remote island in the lower reaches of Barnetuck Bay there lived a family of fisherfolk by the name of Pruitt. There were seven of them, and they were the sole inhabitants of the place. They subsisted on canned corn, canned tomatoes, pressed duck, whole-wheat bread, terrapin, Rice Krispies, crabs, cheese, queen olives, and homemade wild-grape preserve. Once in a while Pa Pruitt made some whiskey and they all had a drink.

They liked the island and lived there from choice. In winter, when there wasn't much doing, they slept the clock around, like so many bears. In summer they dug clams and set off a few pinwheels and salutes on July 4th. No case of acute appendicitis had ever been known in the Pruitt household, and when a Pruitt had a pain in his side he never even noticed whether it was the right side or the left side, but just hoped it would go away, and it did.

One very severe winter Barnetuck Bay froze over and the Pruitt family was marooned. They couldn't get to the mainland by boat because the ice was too thick, and they couldn't walk ashore because the ice was too treacherous. But inasmuch as no Pruitt had anything to go ashore for, except mail (which was entirely second class), the freeze-up didn't make any difference. They stayed indoors, kept warm, and ate well, and when there was nothing better to do, they played crokinole. The winter would have passed quietly enough had not someone on the mainland remembered that the Pruitts were out there in the frozen bay. The word got passed around the county and finally reached the Superintendent of State Police, who immediately notified Pathé News and the United States Army. The Army got there first, with three bombing planes from Langley Field, which flew low over the island and dropped packages of dried apricots and bouillon cubes, which the Pruitts didn't like much. The newsreel plane, smaller than the bombers and equipped with skis, arrived next and landed on a snow-covered field on the north end of the island. Meanwhile, Major Bulk, head of the state troopers, acting on a tip that one of the Pruitt children had appendicitis, arranged for a dog team to be sent by plane from Laconia, New Hampshire, and also dispatched a squad of troopers to attempt a crossing of the bay. Snow began falling at sundown, and during the night three of the rescuers lost their lives about half a mile from shore, trying to jump from one ice cake to another.

The plane carrying the sled dogs was over southern New England when ice began forming on its wings. As the pilot circled for a forced landing, a large meat bone which one of the dogs had brought along got wedged in the socket of the main control stick, and the plane went into a steep dive and crashed against the side of a powerhouse, instantly killing the pilot and all the dogs, and fatally injuring Walter Ringstead, 7, of 3452 Garden View Avenue, Stamford, Conn.

Shortly before midnight, the news of the appendicitis reached the Pruitt house itself, when a chartered autogiro from Hearst's International News Service made a landing in the storm and reporters informed Mr. Pruitt that his oldest boy, Charles, was ill and would have to be taken to Baltimore for an emergency operation. Mrs. Pruitt remonstrated, but Charles said his side did hurt a little, and it ended by his leaving in the giro. Twenty minutes later another plane came in, bearing a surgeon, two trained nurses, and a man from the National Broadcasting Company, and the second Pruitt boy, Chester, underwent an exclusive appendectomy in the kitchen of the Pruitt home, over the Blue Network. This lad died, later, from eating dried apricots too soon after his illness, but Charles, the other boy, recovered after a long convalescence and returned to the island in the first warm days of spring.

He found things much changed. The house was gone, having caught fire on the third and last night of the rescue when a flare dropped by one of the departing planes lodged in a bucket of trash on the piazza. After the fire, Mr. Pruitt had apparently moved his family into the emergency shed which the radio announcers had thrown up, and there they had dwelt under rather difficult conditions until the night the entire family was wiped out by drinking a ten-percent solution of carbolic acid which the surgeon had left behind and which Pa Pruitt had mistaken for grain alcohol.

Barnetuck Bay seemed a different place to Charles. After giving his kin decent burial, he left the island of his nativity and went to dwell on the mainland.

THE HOUR OF LETDOWN

When the man came in, carrying the machine, most of us looked up from our drinks, because we had never seen anything like it before. The man set the thing down on top of the bar near the beerpulls. It took up an ungodly amount of room and you could see the bartender didn't like it any too well, having this big, ugly-looking gadget parked right there.

"Two rye-and-water," the man said.

The bartender went on puddling an Old-Fashioned that he was working on, but he was obviously turning over the request in his mind.

"You want a double?" he asked, after a bit.

"No," said the man. "Two rye-and-water, please." He stared straight at the bartender, not exactly unfriendly but on the other hand not affirmatively friendly.

Many years of catering to the kind of people that come into saloons had provided the bartender with an adjustable mind. Nevertheless, he did not adjust readily to this fellow, and he did not like the machine—that was sure. He picked up a live cigarette that was idling on the edge of the cash register, took a drag out of it, and returned it thoughtfully. Then he poured two shots of rye whiskey, drew two glasses of water, and shoved the drinks in front of the man. People were watching. When something a little out of the ordinary takes place at a bar, the sense of it spreads quickly all along the line and pulls the customers together.

The man gave no sign of being the center of attention. He laid a five-dollar bill down on the bar. Then he drank one of the ryes and chased it with water. He picked up the other rye, opened a small vent in the machine (it was like an oil cup) and poured the whiskey in, and then poured the water in.

The bartender watched grimly. "Not funny," he said in an even voice. "And furthermore, your companion takes up too much room. Why'n you put it over on that bench by the door, make more room here."

"There's plenty of room for everyone here," replied the man.

"I ain't amused," said the bartender. "Put the goddam thing over near the door like I say. Nobody will touch it."

The man smiled. "You should have seen it this afternoon," he said. "It was magnificent. Today was the third day of the tournament. Imagine it—three days of continuous brainwork! And against the top players in the country, too. Early in the game it gained an advantage; then for two hours it exploited the advantage brilliantly, ending with the opponent's king backed in a corner. The sudden capture of a knight, the neutralization of a bishop, and it was all over. You know how much money it won, all told, in three days of playing chess?"

"How much?" asked the bartender.

"Five thousand dollars," said the man. "Now it wants to let down, wants to get a little drunk."

The bartender ran his towel vaguely over some wet spots. "Take it somewheres else and get it drunk there!" he said firmly. "I got enough troubles."

The man shook his head and smiled. "No, we like it here." He pointed at the empty glasses. "Do this again, will you, please?"

The bartender slowly shook his head. He seemed dazed but dogged. "You stow the thing away," he ordered. "I'm not ladling out whiskey for jokestersmiths."

" 'Jokesmiths,' " said the machine. "The word is 'jokesmiths.' "

A few feet down the bar, a customer who was on his third highball seemed ready to participate in this conversation to which we had all been listening so attentively. He was a middle-aged man. His necktie was pulled down away from his collar, and he had eased the collar by unbuttoning it. He had pretty nearly finished his third drink, and the alcohol tended to make him throw his support in with the underprivileged and the thirsty.

"If the machine wants another drink, give it another drink," he said to the bartender. "Let's not have haggling."

The fellow with the machine turned to his new-found friend and gravely raised his hand to his temple, giving him a salute of gratitude and fellowship. He addressed his next remark to him, as though deliberately snubbing the bartender.

"You know how it is when you're all fagged out mentally, how you want a drink?"

"Certainly do," replied the friend. "Most natural thing in the world."

There was a stir all along the bar, some seeming to side with the bartender, others with the machine group. A tall, gloomy man standing next to me spoke up.

"Another whiskey sour, Bill," he said. "And go easy on the lemon juice."

"Picric acid," said the machine, sullenly. "They don't use lemon juice in these places."

"That does it!" said the bartender, smacking his hand on the bar. "Will you put that thing away or else beat it out of here. I ain't in the mood, I tell you. I got this saloon to run and I don't want lip from a mechanical brain or whatever the hell you've got there."

The man ignored this ultimatum. He addressed his friend, whose glass was now empty.

"It's not just that it's all tuckered out after three days of chess," he said amiably. "You know another reason it wants a drink?"

"No," said the friend. "Why?"

"It cheated," said the man.

At this remark, the machine chuckled. One of its arms dipped slightly, and a light glowed in a dial.

The friend frowned. He looked as though his dignity had been hurt, as though his trust had been misplaced. "Nobody can cheat at chess," he said. "Simpossible. In chess, everything is open and above the board. The nature of the game of chess is such that cheating is impossible."

"That's what I used to think, too," said the man. "But there *is* a way."

"Well, it doesn't surprise me any," put in the bartender. "The first time I laid my eyes on that crummy thing I spotted it for a crook."

"Two rye-and-water," said the man.

"You can't have the whiskey," said the bartender. He glared at the mechanical brain. "How do I know it ain't drunk already?"

"That's simple. Ask it something," said the man.

The customers shifted and stared into the mirror. We were all in this thing now, up to our necks. We waited. It was the bartender's move.

"Ask it what? Such as?" said the bartender.

"Makes no difference. Pick a couple big figures, ask it to multiply them together. You couldn't multiply big figures together if you were drunk, could you?"

The machine shook slightly, as though making internal preparations.

"Ten thousand eight hundred and sixty-two, multiply it by ninety-nine," said the bartender, viciously. We could tell that he was throwing in the two nines to make it hard.

The machine flickered. One of its tubes spat, and a hand changed position, jerkily.

"One million seventy-five thousand three hundred and thirty-eight," said the machine.

Not a glass was raised all along the bar. People just stared gloomily into the mirror; some of us studied our own faces, others took carom shots at the man and the machine.

Finally, a youngish, mathematically minded customer got out a piece of paper and a pencil and went into retirement. "It works out," he reported, after some minutes of calculating. "You can't say the machine is drunk!"

Everyone now glared at the bartender. Reluctantly he poured two shots of rye, drew two glasses of water. The man drank his drink. Then he fed the machine its drink. The machine's light grew fainter. One of its cranky little arms wilted.

For a while the saloon simmered along like a ship at sea in calm weather. Every one of us seemed to be trying to digest the situation, with the help of liquor. Quite a few glasses were refilled. Most of us sought help in the mirror—the court of last appeal.

The fellow with the unbuttoned collar settled his score. He walked stiffly over and stood between the man and the machine. He put one arm around the man, the other arm around the machine. "Let's get out of here and go to a good place," he said.

The machine glowed slightly. It seemed to be a little drunk now.

"All right," said the man. "That suits me fine. I've got my car outside."

He settled for the drinks and put down a tip. Quietly and a trifle uncertainly he tucked the machine under his arm, and he and his companion of the night walked to the door and out into the street.

The bartender stared fixedly, then resumed his light housekeeping. "So he's got his car outside," he said, with heavy sarcasm. "Now isn't that nice!"

A customer at the end of the bar near the door left his drink, stepped to the window, parted the curtains, and looked out. He watched for a moment, then returned to his place and addressed the bartender. "It's even nicer than you think," he said. "It's a Cadillac. And which one of the three of them d'ya think is doing the driving?"

THE DECLINE OF SPORT

In the third decade of the supersonic age, sport gripped the nation in an ever-tightening grip. The horse tracks, the ballparks, the fight rings, the gridirons, all drew crowds in steadily increasing numbers. Every time a game was played, an attendance record was broken. Usually some other sort of record was broken, too—such as the record for the number of consecutive doubles hit by left-handed batters in a Series game, or some such thing as that. Records fell like ripe apples on a windy day. Customs and manners changed, and the five-day business week was reduced to four days, then to three, to give everyone a better chance to memorize the scores.

Not only did sport proliferate but the demands it made on the spectator became greater. Nobody was content to take in one event at a time, and thanks to the magic of radio and television nobody had to. A Yale alumnus, class of 1962, returning to the Bowl with 197,000 others to see the Yale-Cornell football game, would take along his pocket radio and pick up the Yankee Stadium, so that while his eye might be following a fumble on the Cornell twenty-two-yard line, his ear would be following a man going down to second in the top of the fifth, seventy miles away. High in the blue sky above the Bowl, skywriters would be at work writing the scores of other major and minor sporting contests, weaving an interminable record of victory and defeat and using the new high-visibility pink news-smoke perfected by Pepsi-Cola engineers. And in the frames of the giant video sets, just behind the goalposts, this same alumnus could watch Dejected win the Futurity before a record-breaking crowd of 349,-872 at Belmont, each of whom was tuned to the Yale Bowl and following the World Series game in the video and searching the sky for further news of events either under way or just completed. The effect of this vast cyclorama of sport was to divide the spectator's attention, over-subtilize his appreciation, and deaden his passion. As the fourth supersonic decade was ushered in, the picture changed and sport began to wane.

A good many factors contributed to the decline of sport. Substitutions in football had increased to such an extent that there were very few fans in the United States capable of holding the players in mind during play. Each play that was called saw two entirely new elevens lined up, and the players whose names and faces you had familiarized yourself with in the first period were seldom seen or heard of again. The spectacle became as diffuse as the main concourse in Grand Central at the commuting hour.

Express motor highways leading to the parks and stadia had become so wide, so unobstructed, so devoid of all life except automobiles and trees that sport fans had got into the habit of traveling enormous distances to attend events. The normal driving speed had been stepped up to ninety-five miles an hour, and the distance between cars had been decreased to fifteen feet. This put an extraordinary strain on the sport lover's nervous system, and he arrived home from a Saturday game, after a road trip of three hundred and fifty miles, glassy-eyed, dazed, and spent. He hadn't really had any relaxation and he had failed to see Czlika (who had gone in for Trusky) take the pass from Bkeeo (who had gone in for Bjallo) in the third period, because at that moment a youngster named Lavagetto had been put in to pinch-hit for Art Gurlack in the bottom of the ninth with the tying run on second, and the skywriter who was attempting to write "Princeton 0–Lafayette 43" had banked the wrong way, muffed the "3," and distracted everyone's attention from the fact that Lavagetto had been whiffed.

Cheering, of course, lost its stimulating effect on players, because cheers were no longer associated necessarily with the immediate scene but might as easily apply to something that was happening somewhere else. This was enough to infuriate even the steadiest performer. A football star, hearing the stands break into a roar before the ball was snapped, would realize that their minds were not on him and would become dispirited and grumpy. Two or three of the big coaches worried so about this that they considered equipping all players with tiny ear sets, so that they, too, could keep abreast of other sporting events while playing, but the idea was abandoned as impractical, and the coaches put it aside in tickler files, to bring up again later.

I think the event that marked the turning point in sport and started it downhill was the Midwest's classic Dust Bowl game of 1985, when Eastern Reserve's great right end, Ed Pistachio, was shot by a spectator. This man, the one who did the shooting, was seated well down in the stands near the forty-yard line on a bleak October afternoon and was so saturated with sport and with the disappointments of sport that he had clearly become deranged. With a minute and fifteen seconds to play and the score tied, the Eastern Reserve quarterback had whipped a long pass over Army's heads into Pistachio's waiting arms. There was no other player anywhere near him, and all Pistachio had to do was catch the ball and run it across the line. He dropped it. At exactly this moment, the spectator—a man named Homer T. Parkinson, of 35 Edgemere Drive, Toledo, O.—suffered at least three other major disappointments in the realm of sport. His horse, Hiccough, on which he had a five-hundred-dollar bet, fell while getting away from the starting gate at Pimlico and broke its leg (clearly visible in the video); his favorite shortstop, Lucky Frimstitch, struck out and let three men die on base in the final game of the Series (to which Parkinson was tuned); and the Governor Dummer soccer team, on which Parkinson's youngest son played goalie, lost to

Kent, 4–3, as recorded in the sky overhead. Before anyone could stop him, he drew a gun and drilled Pistachio, before 954,000 persons, the largest crowd that had ever attended a football game and the *second*-largest crowd that had ever assembled for any sporting event in any month except July.

This tragedy, by itself, wouldn't have caused sport to decline, I suppose, but it set in motion a chain of other tragedies, the cumulative effect of which was terrific. Almost as soon as the shot was fired, the news flash was picked up by one of the skywriters directly above the field. He glanced down to see whether he could spot the trouble below, and in doing so failed to see another skywriter approaching. The two planes collided and fell, wings locked, leaving a confusing trail of smoke, which some observers tried to interpret as a late sports score. The planes struck in the middle of the nearby eastbound coast-to-coast Sunlight Parkway, and a motorist driving a convertible coupé stopped so short, to avoid hitting them, that he was bumped from behind. The pileup of cars that ensued involved 1,482 vehicles, a record for eastbound parkways. A total of more than three thousand persons lost their lives in the highway accident, including the two pilots, and when panic broke out in the stadium, it cost another 872 in dead and injured. News of the disaster spread quickly to other sports arenas and started other panics among the crowds trying to get to the exits, where they could buy a paper and study a list of the dead. All in all, the afternoon of sport cost 20,003 lives, a record. And nobody had much to show for it except one small Midwestern boy who hung around the smoking wrecks of the planes, captured some aero news-smoke in a milk bottle, and took it home as a souvenir.

From that day on, sport waned. Through long, noncompetitive Saturday afternoons, the stadia slumbered. Even the parkways fell into disuse as motorists rediscovered the charms of old, twisty roads that led through main streets and past barnyards, with their mild congestions and pleasant smells.

THE CRACK OF DOOM

Several months prior to the end of the world, the elms died off. The blight which killed them was introduced into this country with a shipment of elm logs consigned to a novelty hat concern, which manufactured funny hats for men's banquets. Within a few weeks, so persistent was the fungus, there was not an elm tree left in the East. The loss, particularly in New England, was regarded as unfortunate but not significant; and the E. I. du Pont de Nemours Company soon brought out a superior funny hat made out of a new substance called Fibrotex. The willows went shortly after.

In almost all parts of the world people began to notice a great increase in rainfall. Boston experienced a precipitation of five inches within twenty-four hours, followed by a long period of drought. Meteorologists, unable to predict the weather with any accuracy, took to writing about it at great length for the papers. It was apparent to everyone that tropical storms were occurring more frequently than in any other period of time within memory. These disturbances were of great violence; they moved farther to the northward and westward than observers had ever noticed before, and in consequence interfered with the plans of a larger number of people.

Coincidental with these atmospheric disturbances was a series of alarming economic disturbances, arising from the increasing irrelevancy of industrial life. The motor-paced bicycle race was characteristic of the inverted activity of the period. The heath hen disappeared, and in isolated sections of the world sleeping sickness broke out. During one of the worst of the storms which ravaged the New Jersey coast, one of the encephalitis victims was offered a large sum if he would allow himself to be exhibited at the Century of Progress Exposition.

Science was making rapid strides. Its findings were of a brilliant rather than a comforting nature, most of them merely demonstrating the futility of earlier scientific advance. In the field of medicine, for example, it was discovered that the gold inlays commonly used by dentists in filling teeth were being gradually absorbed into people's bloodstreams, causing varicose veins. Tularemia, once thought to be the result of the bite of a rabbit, was found to be the result of the widespread use of iodine on cuts and abrasions. A new disease, which began to attack the backs of people's necks in middle life, was traced to the custom (which had come in around 1910) of feeding orange juice to very young babies; doctors found that persons who had been fed orange juice when tiny experienced a stiffening of the muscles of the neck before sixty, making it hard for them to turn around and look behind them. In agriculture, through the use of metallic sprays, fruits and vegetables were brought to a new high point of perfection: an apple was produced as large as a pumpkin, its only disillusioning quality being that it contained enough arsenic residue to kill whoever might eat it.

Radio, even before the elms died, was reaching extraordinary heights. The sounds emitted by studios seeped into houses and even into automobiles. A preponderance of programs advertised products which were "soft" and "smooth," or which made, or tended to make, life itself "soft" and "smooth." Manufacturers of beauty cream said it would make the face softer and smoother. Manufacturers of motor oil said the oil would make one's motor run softly, with greater smoothness. Manufacturers of baking powder said the powder would produce cake of a new, softer, smoother texture. This softness and smoothness of all things in the radio field, coupled with various automatic devices such as self-opening doors and self-running furnaces, contributed only slightly to human happiness, because although many things were softer and smoother, the average person didn't feel well enough to enjoy them.

In the midst of these disturbing manifestations, a research was being conducted by a young man named Elias Gott, in a Norfolk jacket. Mr. Gott was following up the tenable and somber theory that the increase in the number of storms, blights, and floods was caused by radio waves. He had rigged up an observatory in his garage and had proved to his own satisfaction that periods of excessive radio advertising of soft, smooth articles were followed by violent storms, and that the size of the storm area was in direct proportion to the duration of the program and the softness of the product. It was also his belief that the vast increase in broadcasting was causing the earth to deviate from its path around the sun.

In order to complete the experiments by which he hoped to prove this theory, it was necessary for him to make a balloon flight into the stratosphere, carrying delicate instruments. The event awakened national interest; the takeoff, near a dead elm on the outskirts of Batavia, N.Y., was attended by reporters, photographers, and radio announcers in chartered planes. Mr. Gott did not delay. He rose straight and high, quickly outdistancing the planes of the announcers, and disappeared out of sight. When he returned a couple of hours later, he carried with him positive proof that radio waves were causing the earth to veer from its orbit, and that instead of following an elliptical course it wasn't following any particular path at all.

In landing, Gott broke his arm and had to be taken to the Batavia Memorial Hospital; but this minor accident only served to increase the activity of the radio people. NBC dispatched six radio-equipped Curtiss Condors from the Floyd Bennett Airport to Batavia with instructions to dive in formation at the windows of the hospital and give the radio audience a first-hand account of Gott's condition.

"We're going to pick up messages from these planes," said the voice at the studio, "and alternate them with the reports coming through from the bedside, in order to give you the complete details of the wonderful achievement that went on there this afternoon. This is Ted Garnett speaking. Can Robert Tersh hear me? Calling Robert Tersh, piloting the Curtiss Condor Number One from Floyd Bennett Field. If you can hear me, Bob, I wish you would cut in and give the members of the radio audience a little picture of how things look up there in the darkness over the hospital where . . . [Another voice] Tersh speaking, Tersh speaking, here we are in the Number One Condor, we've got six thousand feet under us, and there they are!—the lights of Batavia, twinkling down there in the blackness where Elias Gott, the gamest little flier who ever lived, is lying with a broken arm after his magnificent stratosphere hop . . . [The studio] That was Robert Tersh in the Condor giving you a direct flash from the scene of the Gott flight itself. Wait a minute, now, here's a flash from the bedside, I'll let you have Mike Melcher, who is in the corridor right outside Gott's door. All right, pick it up, Mike. . . . [Another voice] This is Melcher in the Batavia Memorial Hospital, we've set up shop here right outside Gott's door and have just sent in a note reading 'A million congratulations on the magnificent job you did in the cause of scientific achievement' and have received an answer back in Gott's characteristic cryptic style: 'Many thanks for your note, it ought not be long now.' Incidentally, his arm is . . . [The studio] This is Graham McNamee at the studio, we're trying our darndest to pick up Bob Tersh, who is leading the Condors from Floyd Bennett Field; wait a minute, have you got Tersh, Harry? All right, pick it up, Bob! [Voice from the plane] Tersh talking, Tersh talking, we've just completed a series of power dives from three thousand feet at the hospital window, and I want to say before I go any further that this is some night, clear and bright, and every star doing its stuff; and folks, a little note of tragedy has crept into this flight—the last plane of the squadron piloted by Eddie Geer has been reported out. We've just picked up a message from a private operator saying that the plane crashed in thick fog near Elmira. Eddie was killed instantly and I want to say that a gamer little flier never lived . . . [Studio] McNamee speaking, thanks, Bob! We've just had a check on Eddie Geer's magnificent and tragic end in the dense fog near Elmira, and believe me you never saw a sorrier lot of boys than we here at this end of the line. We just picked up the flash a minute ago and already we have sent out two more Condors from the field which are winging their way through the dark this very second to Elmira to the scene of the crash in order to give you first-hand information of the tragic and heroic crackup of Eddie Geer. I'm going to give you back to Mike Melcher, now, at the Batavia Hospital, who will tell you how Gott is."

It was during this broadcast that Elias Gott's theory about the effects of radio waves on the earth's orbit turned out to be correct. The earth, already far off its course, swung wide and loose into the firmament, hit a fixed star, and went up in brilliant flame. The light was noticed on Mars, where it brought a moment of pleasure to young lovers; for on Mars it is the custom to kiss one's beloved when a star falls.